Helen & Scott Nearing.

From the Books of

NORMA AND
WENDELL MANEY

FROM NORMAN LEVINE'S EDITIONS

The Brave New World

THE
BRAVE
NEW
WORLD

by Helen & Scott Nearing

SOCIAL SCIENCE INSTITUTE
HARBORSIDE, MAINE

SALUTATIONS

to the sturdy, bright-eyed children and young people
of the Brave New World
Tomorrow they will be its planners and directors
May they build wisely, usefully, beautifully and well

"O wonder!
How many goodly creatures are there here!
How beauteous mankind is!
O brave new world, that has such people in it!"

The Tempest

CONTENTS

vii

III. SOCIALISM, PEACE AND FRIENDSHIP

PREFACE

Two considerations led us to put time and energy into a trip through the Soviet Union and the People's Republic of China during the winter of 1957-58. The first consideration was a simple matter of time tables. We had spent the previous winter in Canada, South East Asia, the Middle East and Europe. Out of this experience we gathered the material that went into *Socialists Around the World.** Our passports, issued in January, 1956, expired in January, 1958. We felt that we should use the remaining months of passport validity to have a look at the developments in the two countries that were making the most extensive efforts to establish planned and purposed social order and progress.

Our second consideration was a professional one. We often talked and wrote about two of the most experimental and most controversial areas in the world—Russia and China —without any recent first-hand knowledge to fortify our factual background. It was twenty-one years since we had been in the USSR and thirty years since one of us had visited China. We felt that we owed it to our profession, our readers and ourselves to see, hear and feel out these areas at first-hand.

Between the muddling of the British, the fly-by-night irresponsibility of the French and the bungling bellicosity of the State Department, the West seemed hovering on the brink of an experiment in the large-scale use of atomic weapons. We felt that it had made its contribution to human ex-

* N.Y.: Monthly Review Press, 1958.

1

perience and was preparing either to curl up in its corner and pass quietly into the archives of history, or else was getting ready to pop off in a mushrooming cloud of radiant particles. In contrast to this impending calamity we hoped to find in China and Russia evidences of progress, peace and friendship.

We did not go to sit in judgment on the New World. We had neither the mandate nor the experience necessary for such a task. We went to observe and study, to see its activities, to estimate its trends and to evaluate its motive forces. We have done our best to view some of the economic, political and social developments which directly affect the lives of eight or nine hundred million people (and indirectly the lives of other hundreds of millions), to describe them and to compare them with past and present life patterns.

We do not attempt to say the last word concerning the Brave New World. It is growing and changing so rapidly that what was true while these words were written may be superceded by the time they are set in cold type. Those who read our report must take this element of growth or change into consideration whenever they think of the New World or read about its doings. In fact, the most hopeful thing about the New World that we can report is that it is changing, changing fast, and changing for the better.

There are those who go to the Soviet Union and to the People's Republic of China to criticise and find fault. They are on the lookout for sensational shortcomings. Such reporting pays well in the West,—especially in the United States.

There are those who go to check on the political balance, —to find out who is on the way up and who on the way out. Personalities, and the controversies and conflicts in which they engage, make good copy. To gain such information reporters frequent embassies, salons, hotels, cafés, where they can pick up rumors, tips and whispers of intrigue.

There are those who go to Moscow and Peking to gaze at or to meet celebrities and other well-known people, to attend receptions, to catch bits of conversation, and if possible, to interview a top leader.

There are those who are chiefly concerned to seek out the presence or absence of some right or freedom, to compare Russian or Chinese institutions with their opposites in the United States,—almost always to the disadvantage of the foreign country. After a week or two, many such inquirers recross the Atlantic or the Pacific disillusioned and unenlightened.

There are tourists who go to the Soviet Union and to China to see the sights,—to visit palaces, museums, galleries, temples, historical exhibits and other relics of the past. They have neither interest nor inclination to see and share the everyday life of the people.

We went to the Soviet Union and to the People's Republic of China to do none of these things. True, we kept our fingers on the pulse of political affairs. We inquired into rights and freedoms. We attended some parties and went to some museums and exhibits. But chiefly we went to see and be with the people—at work, at play and, wherever possible, in their homes. We went to observe what the people were doing, thinking, planning. We went to find out where they were headed and whether they were succeeding in putting their ideas into practice. We went to see whether the new institutions were advancing the general welfare or whether they were serving the interests of privileged classes. In a word, we went to learn, to see what was going on, to get the developments in proper perspective, and to bring back reports of our observations which would throw some light on parts of the world that have been kept in dark shadow

3

through a deliberate policy of ignoring the new and discrediting the different.

We returned from our winter visit convinced that the peoples of East Europe and Asia have taken the steps necessary to preserve the most valuable of Western culture traits and that they are building these traits (and many of their own improvising) into a culture that will be more humanly advantageous than anything which Westerners have been able to produce.

We came back with still another conviction, of transcendant importance. Peoples cannot build socialism while they are fighting wars. Socialist construction is an absorbing full-time occupation. As Nikita Khrushchev put it on November 6, 1957, "It is a task of unparallelled complexity and difficulty." Having been through terrible ordeals of wholesale destruction and blood-letting, the people of the Soviet Union and China advocate peaceful co-existence and a policy of non-interference in the internal affairs of other countries. Like the three-score-and-ten small, weak nations which make up the majority of the United Nations, the Soviet Union and the People's Republic of China have little to gain and much to lose by hot and cold wars. Their aim is to build socialism and to live at peace with the world.

Reputedly, man is a rational being,—conscious, able to distinguish between himself and his environment. He is endowed with the capacity to compare and contrast different modes of living. He is ingenious, imaginative, persistent, altruistic. He is capable of cooperation and mutual aid on a vast scale and over long periods of time. Above all, he is in a position to transmit to future generations the results of human endeavor and of his own experience. It is high time that a being so richly endowed should devote his energies to the conservation and utilization of natural wealth, the

4

planning and organization of a rational and just society, with particular concern for safeguarding his most precious possession,—the capacities and potentialities of oncoming generations.

Helen and Scott Nearing

Harborside, Maine
June 1, 1958

INTRODUCTION

We bring good news to the people of the West. There is a New World growing up in parts of Europe and Asia. We have seen it, been in it and of it, watched it develop.

Needless to say, the New World is different in many respects from the Old World. Its objectives are new. Its pattern is new. Its ways of life are new.

People who visit the Soviet Union and the People's Republic of China must expect to find attitudes, activities and institutions which differ more or less fundamentally from their counterparts in other countries, particularly in the West. Visitors should be prepared to observe and evaluate differences between their own and alien life patterns, not so much in terms of their own backgrounds, as in terms of the historic situations out of which the alien patterns grew.

One well-known United States liberal, a staunch advocate of civil liberties, returned from his first visit to the Soviet Union discouraged and disillusioned. Reviewing his experiences, he said in a public address: "The Soviet Union has let me down!" Over the years he had formed his opinion of a New World that should tally with his viewpoint and not contradict his own social heritage. After seeing the Soviet reality he was dissatisfied and disappointed because it did not correspond with his expectations. In taking such a position he overlooked the obvious fact that the builders of socialism in the Soviet Union were not aiming to please United States liberals. Their primary task was to set up a social structure

7

which would meet the domestic and international problems confronting their country and its peoples.

Those who visit the Soviet Union or China or any other foreign country must take the local situation into account and use it as a basis of judgment. If they were deciding whether or not to migrate to Russia or China and live there, their own approach to its life and problems would be of paramount importance. Then they could legitimately ask themselves: "How would *I* fit into that social situation? Would *I* feel at home? Could *I* be an adjusted and useful citizen in such a society?" Under such circumstances an egocentric approach to a different social environment would be justified. But a report on social situations which differ from those to which the reporter is accustomed gains in value and importance in direct ratio to the ability of the reporter to put himself in the places of those about whom he is reporting. Are they in good health? Are they adjusted, balanced human beings? Does their society meet their needs and fulfill their hopes and aspirations?

Some problems are common to people everywhere. At the same time, each people faces issues which are peculiar to its particular cultural level and its economic and political background. In that sense the attitudes, outlooks and institutions of each people must be evaluated in terms of the situation out of which they have developed. A visitor to another country must be prepared to examine that area from the viewpoint of the host country, and with some understanding of its history.

Rivalry and conflict between Tsarist Russia and her neighbors in Europe and Asia are part and parcel of modern history. Russian policy in the Baltic, in the Black Sea area and in the Far East led to wars with Germany, Britain, Turkey, Japan—wars of rivalry and imperial ambition. Differ-

8

ences between the economic, political and social patterns of these countries (and their contemporaries) aggravated misunderstandings and pointed toward conflict. But in certain respects, all of these countries had similar objectives and parallel social systems. All were monarchies, in various stages of industrialization. All had similar property and class structures. All were expanding in search of raw materials and markets. All maintained strong military establishments. All were prepared to use war as an instrument of policy. Contradictions and antagonisms were normal aspects of the capitalist imperialist struggle to divide and redivide the world.

Bolshevism, or communism as it is now called, introduced a new factor into the historical picture, pushing imperialist rivalries into second place and establishing a new type of rivalry, presently called the cold war.

Events leading up to the Bolshevik seizure of power in 1917 involved a break with the past. The Russian Revolution was no palace coup, nor was it a struggle between rivals having the same class origin. It was a social revolution in the true sense of that term because it threw overboard established goals, purposes, outlooks, practices and institutions, and replaced them by new culture traits and a new culture pattern.

Social revolution was not confined to Russia. Its beginnings may be traced back into the middle of 19th century Europe. During the years following 1917, the teachings of communism have been accepted by peoples in various parts of Europe and Asia. But the most dramatic breaks with the past and the most spectacular attempts to establish a culture pattern which would equal, excel and finally replace capitalism have been made in the Soviet Union and the People's Republic of China.

9

Concepts of both theory and practice separated the new order in these countries from the old one. Foremost among the purposes of the communists was the ending of exploitation through the social ownership of natural resources, including land, and the social ownership of those means of production which enabled the owners to live without labor on the goods and services produced by others.

Competition for wealth and power was to be replaced by cooperative relationships in which specialization and division of labor would increase productivity and the product would be divided in the early stages according to production, and later, according to need.

Social revolutions open the way for social pioneers to blueprint and build new patterns of culture. A collective economy and society must be planned by social scientists and engineers who work out a rational theory and practice of social organization which will promote the general welfare.

Social ownership, cooperation and social planning run counter to the accepted theories of capitalist imperialism. Peoples who choose social ownership, cooperation and social planning, reject private ownership, competition and the wealth-power struggle.

National boundaries and nationalism hold a dominant place in capitalist theory and practice. Socialism, on the contrary, cannot be confined within national frontiers. Eventually it must take in the entire human family, freeing the colonial peoples and setting them on the highway to nationhood and self-determination.

New ideas, practices and institutions do not spring fully matured from historical situations. Rather they mature and ripen in the course of historical experiences. Those who undertake to plan and guide historical processes are pioneers in the true sense of that term,—blazing untrod paths and inaugurating hitherto unknown means for achieving the life and well-being which all peoples seek.

We had left a Western world in which invention and discovery had enlarged man's control over nature and greatly extended the possibility of establishing a rational society, of providing abundance, of abolishing war and promoting peace and good will among all members of the human family. Yet these enlarged and extended controls over nature and society were being used to make rich men richer, powerful men more powerful, and, as an ultimate act of folly and wickedness, to destroy life and property wholesale in a series of fratricidal, suicidal wars.

We found ourselves in a New World which rejected the private ownership of the means of production, repudiated the competitive struggle for wealth and power as a dangerous and pernicious policy, and attempted to utilize man's control over nature and his greatly extended possibilities of planning, organizing and directing social relations to provide the best things in life for the greatest number of people.

Turning its back upon the tradition of private ownership of the sources of livelihood and the custom of guaranteeing to a privileged few preferred access to the goods and services produced by the many, the New World we visited was experimenting with a social pattern which distributed income in proportion to productive effort, with special provisions for those who, because of considerations beyond their personal control, were less able than their fellows to play a productive role in society.

Such a world was not only new. It also aimed to be rational by equalizing opportunity, recognizing and encouraging special ability, universalizing education, promoting science and scientific research, conserving natural resources, increasing productive capacity and enlarging the participation of the citizenry in the planning and direction of economic, political and social affairs.

We thanked our lucky stars for the chance to visit this New World and we eagerly accept this and every other opportunity to bring to the attention of our fellow citizens some of the more important among its aspects and activities.

PART ONE

"The dog barks, but the caravan moves on."

Azerbaijan Proverb

1. A NEW WORLD IN THE MAKING

We ran into beggars almost everywhere during our previous winter's journey through the Middle East, South and West Asia. In some places they buzzed about us as flies buzz around a drop of honey. We had something; they wanted it. They held out their hands, appealing with every artifice at their command. Some of these mendicants were tottering on the edge of the grave. Some of them were hardly out of the cradle. It was a harrowing experience to face need, dire poverty and semi-starvation at almost every turn. These fellow humans were asking for something; they had nothing to give in return. They were destitute, and to them we looked wealthy. "Something for nothing," they pleaded.

This is the social life pattern of a large part of the Old World: get without giving. The beggars live by that system; so do the rich. The beggars live off hand-outs, and the rich live on rent, dividends and other unearned income. The ethics of the Old World is based on the formula: Get all you can for as little as you can, and where possible, get something for nothing.

Early in November, 1957, we found ourselves, together with a considerable number of other fog-bound travelers, in the Prague airport. Among us were people from many nations and from every continent. Long-robed, dark-skinned Africans; small-boned and delicate Koreans and Burmese; turbanned Hindus and Nepalese were held up for days, together with Italians, French, Australians, Britishers and a few Americans.

Prague is in Czechoslovakia, a part of the socialist New World. Two distinctive Nepalese, Old Worlders, sauntered along a road nead the airport. We saw them pause beside a group of playing children who stopped their game and gathered, chattering and excited, around the strangers, attracted by their unusual attire. The Nepalese felt called upon to make a friendly gesture. They held out something the children had never seen before—Nepalese coins. The children danced up and down but made no effort to grab the money. One Nepalese handed a coin to a small boy who fingered it eagerly and then gave it back. "Take it," said the Nepalese, holding out the coin again. The boy looked longingly, then turned and ran away, to his mother, who was standing with other women not a great way off. In a moment he was back, with a Czech coin of equal size. This he handed to the Nepalese and then gladly took the strange money in return. The Nepalese tried again with another coin. Each child who wanted a foreign coin found one of his own to offer in exchange.

With our Asian experience fresh in mind we watched the little drama with great interest and some astonishment. Here were strangers in the Prague streets trying to give away money. No child would take until he was able to make an exchange. Here was something for something, not something for nothing, as was the case in the Old World.

We wondered whether this incident in the Prague street was a chance episode, or was it something new under the sun? During the weeks that followed, as we penetrated more deeply into the New World, we saw this drama of something for something repeated again and again. Not one beggar did we see in the socialist countries. We saw youngsters (especially in Moscow) on the street, in schools, outside the hotels, eager for coins, postage stamps, pins, momentoes,—but only on

16

condition that they could return something of equal value.

The *New York Times* of March 3, 1958, reported an interview with Blanche Thebom, the Metropolitan Opera singer, who visited the Soviet Union in the winter of 1957. "It was the children, with their excellent manners, their fairness and direct ways, that completely won Miss Thebom. . . . In Kiev, Miss Thebom encountered, as she did in the other cities, crowds of children who wanted to trade coins. On the edge of the crowd, she noticed a little boy who appeared very anxious to trade but obviously had come without his Russian coins. When Miss Thebom tried to give him some coppers, he refused, saying that 'it would not be fair.' Finally, she persuaded him to surrender a pin he wore as a suitable barter."

On another and higher level we found the same principle operating. The people everywhere in the socialist countries were eager and avid to take an active part in the life of their homes, schools, organizations, state or country, offering their energy, talents and capacities. In return they reaped rich rewards in education, better living conditions and security. Here was the same consistent pattern of something for something repeated throughout a whole society. At length we were convinced. We were in a New World. Something for something was part of its ethic.

Citizens of the Soviet Union celebrated the fortieth anniversary of their October, 1917, Revolution on November 7, 1957. Officially the celebrations lasted for three days. Actually there were several days before and after November 7 when the parents and children of the Russian Revolution spent their time going to meetings and parties, putting up flags, banners and slogans, parading or watching others march and demonstrate. Thousands of out-of-town visitors streamed in from neighboring villages and cities, and came from every continent and a hundred foreign countries to offer their

17

congratulations and wish the Union of Socialist Soviet Republics long life and success in its strenuous efforts to build peace, friendship and socialism.

Those who were so fortunate as to join the November demonstrations will not soon forget the masses of bright-faced, warmly dressed women, men, young folks and children who thronged the well-paved, clean, decorated, flood-lighted streets, joining in the demonstrations, clapping, cheering, singing, dancing, slapping each other on the back and kissing on both cheeks, Russian fashion.

War ruins and the relics of Tsarist Russia's backwardness had largely disappeared. In their place, on all sides we saw planned purpose, order and cleanliness. Old Moscow had been a grimey, slow-moving, almost sleepy city. Moscow in 1957 was shining, vibrating and pulsating with life.

Soviet people were certainly happy and proud on November 7th. Forty years earlier they had begun to convert a shattered Tsarist government, a broken-down economy, a community torn by civil war and a country occupied and encircled by foreign armies, into a unified, compact, socialist society. They had expelled the interventionists, defeated the counter-revolution, rebuilt old cities and constructed new ones, organized and collectivized the vast countryside. They had written their 1918 constitution declaring an end to exploitation, launched the 1920 Fifty Year Program to electrify the entire country, and in 1928 inaugurated their First Five Year Plan. Between 1941 and 1945 they had met and repulsed armies backed by the productive capacity of half of Europe.

There had been eight world powers in 1917. In 1945 there were two, and one of them was the 28 year old Soviet Union. Most of the war damage was repaired by 1950. After that, new construction proceeded in giant strides. The Soviet people had paused to hurl back the invaders from the West, and then had thrown themselves with boundless enthusiasm and renewed determination into the task of building social- ism. The results of their efforts gratified and amazed the visitors who journeyed to Moscow in November, 1957.

Except for a few grizzled, decorated veterans who were being patted on the back, toasted and photographed because they had taken part in the struggles of October, 1917, most of the people we saw had either been born since the Revolu- tion or were too young to remember the stirring events of that period. We were meeting a new generation—the children of October. These children of the revolution had passed through the terrible ordeal of 1941-45 and had come through unafraid and undismayed by the immensity of the tasks con- fronting them. They had tended the wounded, buried the dead, cleared away the wreckage, studied, planned and re- built, reaching heights of achievement undreamed of in 1920 and 1928.

Certainly among the most enthralling sights during the celebrations were the small children. Moscow is cold in early November. Snow and ice were in the streets before the month was over. The winds were bitter. We saw children everywhere, thousands of them, and not one looked cold, not one neglected. The adults were warmly clothed. But without exception the children who accompanied them were better dressed than their elders. The rosy-faced tiny tots were frequently bundled in fur. Many were so well-wrapped that they could roll more easily than toddle.

Children and young people in the Soviet Union seem neither petted nor spoiled, though they are greatly loved. They are healthy, up-standing and self-reliant. They feel secure and confident, and radiate friendliness and good cheer. They have a part to play in society; they know where they are going, and they are on their way. The forty years of

19

revolution and pioneering have produced a fine new crop of Soviet citizens.

Most school children in the USSR of 9 to 14 years of age hope to join the Young Pioneers and wear the orange-red scarf which is the Pioneer badge of membership. When joining the Pioneers "the pupil undertakes to fulfil the pledge of the Young Pioneer, to study diligently, be disciplined, courteous and industrious, to respect the labor of others, to protect everything that belongs to the people, to take part in social work, to be honest and truthful, to help his parents, to respect his elders and to look after younger children, to go in for physical training and sports." *

Being a Pioneer carries with it a certain distinction. There are notable advantages, such as camping trips, sports tournaments, participation in public functions, and the possibility of attending the Pioneer Houses after school to play and to learn. There are over 2,000 Pioneer Houses where the playrooms, toys, tools and books, the social events and the courses of study are all free, the funds being provided by the trade unions and city authorities. About 18 million boys and girls belonged to the Young Pioneers in January, 1958, and were happily spending their spare time at these Pioneer Houses, learning while they were being amused and entertained.

Districts in every city or town have Pioneer Houses. In many of the largest cities of the Soviet Union they are called Pioneer Palaces. Palace is a word often used in Russia to designate a large building (such as Palace of Culture, Palace of Labor). In some cases the Young Pioneer headquarters are palaces in fact as well as in name. The Pioneer Palace in Leningrad, where 10,000 school children can go, is a good example. Here the Empress Maria, mother of the last Tsar,

* Deineko, M., *Public Education in the USSR*, 1956.

had lived in a huge building which in 1943 was turned over to the Young Pioneers of Leningrad.

We spent an exhilarating afternoon there, pulled from room to room by little girls who were anxious that we see every corner of their 400-room palace playhouse. Not only were the children (about 3,000 on the day of our visit) playing games, dancing in a great hall and singing together, but they were studying and working in small groups. We saw ballet classes, calisthenic courses, sewing circles, a painting class, boys working in a tool shop, others in a planetarium with exhibits of sputniks and of the heavens. We were tip-toed into a quiet library and to a chessroom where children were sitting silently absorbed in their games. In another room twenty very small children were sitting on a sumptuous rug in a glistening-chandeliered boudoir of the late Empress, listening to fairy stories.

In the Pioneer Palace of Stalingrad we saw similar activities. Sculpture and oil painting were being taught in studios. Children were working a puppet theatre of their own. Girls of 13 to 17 were busy at sewing machines in a dressmaking class. Boys were building model boats. In a dancing class we came on a score of little girls in white slips who were specializing in folk dances of all countries. They showed us their beautifully illustrated 750 page book of folk dances, said they intended to learn them all, and demonstrated a Highland Fling for us.

Pioneer headquarters offer millions of Soviet children opportunities to spend their spare time pursuing one or another line of interest under expert guidance. If new interests crop up, the responsible leaders of the Pioneer movement aim to satisfy them. The Pioneer centers offer classes in plane building and competitions in flying their home-made planes. The growth of radio and television have led to the development

21

of laboratories in both of these fields. Now that Soviet industry is producing an abundance of reasonably-priced cameras, Pioneer groups are organized to take, develop and exhibit photographs. In a Pioneer Palace in Baku an excited group of little boys got us into their small studio and, with cameras and flash-bulbs in hand, hopped on chairs and squatted on the floor to get the right angles for our photographs.

In the same Palace was a special Room of International Friendship. Here were displayed all the gifts and letters and magazines from children in foreign lands. One of the most important aspects of Pioneer work is the establishment and maintenance of relations with girls and boys in other countries. Letters, photographs and stamps are exchanged. Exhibits are sent back and forth. Gifts are offered across the frontiers. Thus the Pioneer movement is international culturally, if not yet organizationally.

Young people are not the only pioneers in the Soviet Union. Women by tens of millions are following new paths toward a new life. In Tsarist Russia the bulk of womankind was confined to home and family and personal matters. They had no political rights and little schooling. The 1897 census showed that only 24 percent of the population could read and write, with women's literacy only 12 percent. The rare opportunity of attending institutions or schools of higher learning was reserved for well-to-do women. There was crushing serfdom for women peasants, and for poor women in the towns and cities the same slavery to work. Women were supposed to be home creatures, vassals or playthings of husbands, with little time or opportunity for anything beyond their own small circle of family chores and neighborhood contacts.

Today Soviet women's horizons are unrecognizably enlarged. The sun of freedom and equality has risen on Women's Day in the USSR. There is no limit to what they can achieve and do. They are equals in the home and in society. Article 122 of the Constitution of the USSR grants women "equal rights with men in all spheres of economic, government, cultural, political, and other public activity." Women are using these new rights to gain recognition in widespread fields of science, politics, education, art and industry. Women are reaching and filling high positions throughout the country and more and more playing important roles in government and public affairs.

We met with three officials of the Women's Committee of the Soviet Union, a representative grouping of leaders from the trade union organizations, cooperatives and housewive's leagues. They told us of specific positions women hold in the Soviet Union today. There are women mayors, women heads of factories, women physicists, women directors of schools as well as women station masters, women welders, women lathe operators, women electricians. Women are playing a dominant role in key professions: for example, forty percent of the judges are women; seventy-one percent of the students in medical colleges are women; half the liberal professions, according to recent statistics, are in their hands. Women are prominent in the fields of technical sciences, history, philology, oriental studies. Tens of thousands are doing scientific work in universities, institutes and academies.

Women head important ministries in the USSR: Deputy Chairman of the Council of Ministers; Minister of Culture; Minister of Health; Minister of Social Security; Vice-Minister of Education; Secretary of the Parliamentary Group of the USSR; Deputy People's Commissar of Railways of the USSR; Secretary of the Moscow Central Committee of the Communist Party; Secretary of the Central Committee of the

USSR Communist Party. From the smallest Republic of Moldavia to the largest, the Russian Federation, women occupy prominent positions. In Latvia, the head of the Ministry of Justice is a woman. In Armenia and in the North Ossetian Autonomous Republic women are Ministers of Finance. Nine Kirghiz women are deputies to the Supreme Soviet of the USSR and 112 are deputies to the Supreme Soviet of the Kirghiz Republic. Eight women are Ministers and Deputy Ministers in Kirghiz, with six thousand women chairmen of collective farms, team or group leaders.

To show their achievements in science and education we quote from *Equality of Women in the USSR,* a handbook published in 1957 by the Foreign Languages Publishing House in Moscow. "The scientific personnel of the USSR Academy of Sciences includes 5,795 women, who make up 42.3 percent of the total. . . . More than 100 women head research institutes or laboratories. Over 39,000 (or more than 30 percent of the total number of instructors) are engaged in scientific instruction in Soviet colleges and universities. As many as 96 college directors and deputy directors in charge of scientific instruction, and also 193 faculty deans, are women. . . . There is no longer any scientific field where Soviet women are not working." (pp. 285-6) "At Moscow University alone, upwards of 1,000 women are employed as instructors or research workers, including 32 doctors and more than 470 candidates of various sciences, among them 27 professors and 155 assistant professors." (p. 291) "In our publishing houses and editorial offices the percentage of women is 53.7; in the book trade, 79.8. In the administrative bodies, that is, in the Ministry of Culture of the Russian Federation, the ministries of the autonomous republics, the departments of culture of the regions, territories and districts, the percentage of women is 47.6. In the Ministry of

24

Culture of the RSFSR, key posts are held by 192 women, of whom 17 are department heads." (p. 294)

We asked our friends of the Women's Committee about the purposes of their organization. "In our country we need not fight for equal rights," they said. "We have them. Our tasks are different. We aim, among other things, to establish connection with women in other countries. We are affiliated with 66 countries through the World Federation of Women. We invite women delegates here and send women abroad. Six women doctors went to the USA last month. A return trip will be made by American women doctors. On May 1st twenty American women met and interviewed Premier Bulganin. We remember they asked him for the recipe of his favorite soup! We advise the government on women's problems. Due to our pressure, the 77 days of pregnancy leave are now extended to 112 days, with full pay. We are trying to shorten the working hours on Saturdays and holidays. We advise light industry to produce better quality articles or more useful 'gadgets' to lighten women's house work. We edit a magazine *Soviet Women* which is translated into 10 languages. There are also 18 women's magazines in the USSR."

The coming of Women's Day in the USSR has not only opened up useful careers for women and allowed them to play a prominent role in their country's affairs, it has provided a broader base for their home life by giving many of them a cash income they never had before. With equal pay for equal work and more than one member of the family earning, women have more money to spend. What do they do with their extra earning power? Like women the world over they want comforts for their families and their homes. And with good-looking clothes and accessories they want to enhance their appearance. Never under-estimate the powers

25

of women; their demands are being met in modern Russia.

When we were in the Soviet Union in the late 1920s and 1930s, supplies of other than the necessities of food and clothing were not abundant. Russian stores twenty years ago had few goods in the windows and relatively little inside to buy. People queued up at all hours to purchase any items for sale. There was plenty of bread and the ordinary food stuffs, but luxury items and clothes, notions, dry goods or house furnishings were scarce. They were not yet being produced in sufficient quality to more than tickle the market.

In 1957-58 we saw many more stores and they were bulging with consumer goods and jammed with eager buyers. Western merchants would rejoice if such crowds, with ready money in their pockets, filled their stores. We found it hard to enter shops; we waited three-deep to buy, and had to struggle out against the incoming stream of shoppers. The windows of our hotel room in Moscow faced Gorki Street, a major shopping avenue. Any hour of the day, and way into the night (for many stores are open till 8 and some till 10 PM), crowds of people, reminiscent of 34th Street and Broadway in New York at Christmastime, poured along the streets and over the crossings. And this, our friends said, was typical not only of holiday time but every day, week and month in the year. Whatever the value of the ruble for the foreigner, Soviet citizens have plenty to spend and do not seem to find the prices beyond their purses. The customers do not come to finger and depart. They pull out rolls of rubles and snap up goods from the counters and shelves as soon as they can get near them.*

* A glimpse at the rising standard of living and increasing purchasing power in the USSR can be found in "How Soviet People Live" by Y. Manevich, in *The Land of Soviets,* Moscow: Foreign Languages Publishing House, 1957. "In view of the constantly increasing productivity, output is steadily expanding and costs are falling. That makes it possible to raise living stand-

The food stores are probably the most crammed with products and buyers. Cheese, pastry, vegetables, meat, bread, icecream (to which the Russians are as addicted as Americans) all have their special stores, and all are crowded. Their well-decorated windows glitter and shine with attractively packaged goods. No longer, as in 1935, did we see small apples, wizened oranges and a few boxes of biscuits in a drab shop window. The food shop windows and stores in Moscow would be a credit to any first-class specialty shop in New York City.

The clothing situation is not yet on as high a level, but it also is out of sight of twenty years ago. When we went to Russia the winter of 1957-58 we picked our travelling clothes for warmth and comfort, not for style. The women we met in the USSR this time did not appreciate our old clothes. In certain cases they almost seemed to resent them. Certainly the girl lift-operators in the Ukraine Hotel where we stayed in Moscow were better dressed than we were and there was almost scorn in their swift appraisal of our dowdy clothes. How their eyes were caught and glistened when they saw something new and stylish!

We had two girl interpreters during our five week stay in Moscow. Both were well-dressed. One of the girls designed her own attractive dresses, suits and coats and had them made

---

ards uninterruptedly" (p. 192). "Today, consumption is much higher than in 1940. According to data obtained from a budget survey by the Central Board of Statistics, in 1956 per capita consumption in the families of factory, office and other workers registered the following increases over the 1940 level: meat and fat—by 62 percent; fish and fish products—by 92 percent; milk and other dairy products—by more than 100 percent; eggs—by 86 percent; sugar—by 87 percent. . . . Fabric sales registered a mean increase of 94 percent; leather footwear sales increased by 83 percent" (pp. 194-5). "In 1955, the retail trade turnover in the country was (in comparative prices) almost double that of 1950. The purchasing power of the people is growing so fast that it is overtaking the output of consumer goods. For that reason, the demand for some commodities is not yet being fully supplied" (p. 196).

to fit. The other turned up every day in a new outfit. We counted five different coats she wore in the three weeks she was with us.

The new women in the USSR do not want foreigners to dress down to them. The increasing supplies of consumer goods allow them to buy more clothes and to have more choice in quality, colors, cut and style than ever before. One now sees bright colored garments in the streets, even in winter, instead of the more somber hues we had seen before. Materials are good and furs are worn by many. Hosts of youngsters are bundled in white sheepskin coats and hoods, looking like millionaire's children. Men's hats are heavily furred. Their overcoats are warm and of good quality. Everyone is well shod, which is a great change from twenty years ago.

We went to operas and ballets and theatres in half a dozen cities of the USSR. In Moscow and Leningrad a large proportion of the women in the audiences were well and carefully dressed by Western standards. Two attractive women of our acquaintance were our companions at dinner and the ballet. One taught in the Leningrad Conservatoire. Her smooth blonde hair, peaches and cream complexion, her smart rose-colored blouse and slim black silk skirt would have let her pass for a Parisienne anywhere. Her friend, a strapping woman, a competent executive and mother of two growing girls, had glowing auburn hair stunningly offset by her deep purple dress and violet scarf. These women would have shone in any company.

One of our girl interpreter friends travelled with Blanche Thebom from Moscow to Leningrad and to Kiev, where the American mezzo-soprano gave performances and saw the country and people. She reiterated what the *New York Times* reported: "The singer was delighted to see how 'clothes conscious' Russian women were. . . . In all three cities she found the women exceptionally well-dressed, although hardly fashionable in Parisian terms. 'There just isn't any stigma attached to being over-weight,' she explained." *

Russian women are on the whole larger and bigger-boned than many Europeans and Americans and will always dress differently. Their own taste as to color and style will be worked out to fit their stature and figure. The pulled-back hair and knot and the high crown of braids of older times is being superceded by trim hair-cuts. Beauty parlors are full of women getting permanent waves. Perfume, cosmetic and nylon counters are popular in every department store. Women's taste for novelty and show are being gratified in the Soviet Union. Personally, we have our doubts as to the importance of high style, jewelry, make-up and elaborate hair dress, but if Soviet women want these things they will get them.

We emphasize this point of dress to show that women in the Soviet Union, for all their political complexion, can be as feminine as their sisters in the West. They too are human beings. We are reminded of a story Anna Louise Strong told on one of her trips back to the United States. She had spent many years in the USSR and was giving a talk on "Women in the Soviet Union." She had spoken of their increasing importance in the country, of their equal status with men, of their accomplishments, of the care they received during pregnancy, confinement and child birth, and all of the benefits enjoyed by women in the Soviet Union. After her talk, a woman rose in the audience and asked, "Miss Strong, what you have said was very interesting, but what about those dreadful Bolsheviks?"

* March 3, 1957.

There is no mark of the beast on the women of the Soviet Union. We met women "Bolsheviks" all over the country,—personable, competent, useful members of society. They are living happy, full, productive lives. Socialism is bringing them equal opportunity with men and equal opportunity among women of the whole world. Women's Day is wide open in the Soviet Union today.

2. STEPS IN THE EDUCATIONAL LADDER

Immediately after the Russian Revolution of 1917, unlettered and untutored people flocked into the universities. "We want to know," they said to the professors. "Teach us!"

Alas for the people! What the universities had to offer was far removed from the day-to-day lives of Russian workers. Besides, the universities were designed to meet the needs of students who had spent years in preparatory schools. So the first mass assault on the universities came to an untimely end. An entire generation was to pass before there could be a successful mass movement into the institutions of higher learning.

Soviet policy makers and Soviet educators faced three problems: first, training an adequate number of competent scientists, engineers and technicians; second, planning and building socialism; third, providing educational opportunities which would meet the requirements of a developing socialist community and the personal needs of all who entered the schools.

Preparations for mass education were made along three lines. The first need was buildings and equipment. The second was a corps of trained teachers. The third was sufficient educational opportunities in the school program to meet the varied interests and requirements of the tens of millions of Russian children who were destined to take their places in Soviet schools during the next forty years.

At the time of the Revolution there were some 7 million Russian children in the schools, with 280,000 teachers. Today the number of pupils has risen to 35 million and the teaching staff to 1,811,000. The Russian schools of 1917 were not merely insufficient in number and capacity. They were neglected, ill-equipped and, by any recognized educational standard, backward. The Russian schools of today are meeting the full educational requirements of an entire generation of Soviet children and young people. Schools, built by the tens of thousands (and destroyed by thousands during the invasion of 1941-45), have been restored, equipped, enlarged, multiplied. Universal seven year schooling has been achieved through the immense Soviet countryside, with attendance increased 320 times above that of 1941. Ten year schools are the rule in the cities and will be extended to the rural areas in the near future.

Today the Soviet Union has some 213,000 general educational schools, 35,000 secondary schools and nearly 4,000 professional and technical schools. The general educational, professional and technical schools have a combined attendance of 35 million pupils, but if all categories, such as kindergartens, adult evening classes and correspondence courses were counted, the number would be nearer 50 million. The Soviet Union has about 60,000 pre-school institutions,—nurseries, nursery schools and kindergartens, which care for more than two million children; and nearly 10,000 extra-curricular institutions for children,—Pioneer Houses, centers for young naturalists and technicians, clubs and park centers.

Other requirements which are at least as important as buildings and equipment are a staff of competent teachers in the schools and a teacher-training program that will provide personnel for the expanding educational system. Teacher training courses, now housed chiefly in pedagogical institutes, are to be found in every important city in each of the 15 republics composing the Soviet Union. These 905 pedagogical institutes, with their 800,000 students, are graduating the flood of teachers who make up the two million personnel of the Soviet educational system. Beside their excellent training, all teachers get a month's vacation with pay, wage increases every five years of service. Their trade unions have centers in and out of cities, with facilities such as club rooms, gymnasiums, swimming pools, stadiums and countless cultural activities. They have social security, free medical and dental care. Rural school teachers get free housing.

Enough school rooms to supply every child with a place, and competent teachers in modest plenty, do not satisfy the requirements of a modern educational system. There must be special schools or courses of training to meet every demand. Soviet educational institutions offer instruction for the professions and for all of the standard occupations. Specialized training is provided in technicums, in conservatoires, in art schools, and, for those who cannot attend regular schools, in evening schools and courses by correspondence.

The entire educational apparatus should be within the reach of every child who desires to enter it. Elementary education in Russia is compulsory and free. Higher schooling is voluntary and free. Soviet education has been made free from the bottom to the top of the educational ladder.

Not only is tuition free for any Soviet citizen who wants an education, from day nursery and kindergarten to institute and university, but four-fifths of the students in Soviet higher educational institutions receive scholarships which cover board and lodging and incidental educational expenses.

All Soviet citizens, of both sexes, of all ages, of every racial stock and of every faith, may climb the educational ladder as far as they are able. A complete description of this ladder would begin with the network of nurseries, nursery schools and kindergartens which have been established in all parts of the Soviet Union. The many nurseries and kindergartens we saw were well-run, clean, attractive, well-staffed and well-equipped. They were filled with chubby, cheery little boys and girls who were a delight to see playing, eating, exercising and resting. They all looked a credit to the institutions, and the institutions seemed worthy of them.

The primary unit of Soviet education is the ten year school, which takes children at seven years and aims to graduate them at seventeen. Ten year schools are now generally established in Soviet cities and in many rural areas. In some rural districts there are still only seven year schools; in some there are both ten and seven year schools.

Ten year schools teach literature, civics, history, geography, mathematics, physics, chemistry, biology, secondary languages and the basic language (which is usually Russian, but which may be the language of one of the 58 linguistic groups which make up the Union of Soviet Republics). In addition to these academic subjects, the ten year school offers training in health and physical well being, in sport, in domestic arts, handicrafts, music and the fine arts.

Ten year schools in the cities are likely to be of moderate size, from twenty to forty classes, with thirty to forty children in each class. Because of a shortage of schools and classrooms, many of these primary school units are used twice each day, by a morning and an afternoon shift.

Ten year schools aim to provide a general education for

33

all children and to prepare students for institutes and universities. Pupils who do not intend to continue their studies through higher educational institutions may leave the primary schools at the fifth or the seventh year and enter technicums, or trade schools, which provide specialized training.

Paralleling the ten year schools, classes and schools are organized to which students showing special aptitudes for drawing, music, dancing, sport, mechanics, may go in regular school time, so long as their school work is up to grade standard. Or the students may be transferred to these specialized schools, where they supplement the regular course of study by special work in the field of their aptitude or choice.

During our stay in the Soviet Union we visited a number of ten year schools, which varied somewhat in size and quality. Everywhere we were impressed by the fine work which directors, teachers and pupils were doing. Beyond and above this excellence we were delighted with the human output— the children and young people who were growing up healthy, sturdy, clear-eyed, self-respecting, and confident of themselves and their future.

Early in our Moscow stay we visited a ten year school presided over by a veteran teacher-principal who had devoted most of her adult years to school work. The school was a work of art and a joy for educationalists to see. The principal went anywhere and everywhere, quietly and unobtrusively. The teachers were competent, skilled and in complete control of themselves and their classes. The students went about their routine affairs with interest and absorbed attention. Hardly a head lifted as we entered and left their classrooms. However, they were human children, not robots. Between classes, on the playground and in the gymnasium, we saw them explode with gusto. The school vibrated and tingled with enthusiasm, both at work and at play, but its chief attribute was self-discipline.

Classes in the lower grades were directed by one teacher in one classroom. In the more advanced years, pupils went to special classrooms for special teachers. Subjects like physics, chemistry and biology were taught in well-equipped laboratories by specialists in each field. Work-shops were under the direction of craftsmen in wood, metal and mechanics. The school had a good gymnasium and an auditorium.

Beyond the physical appointments, and completely overshadowing them in this school (and all schools we visited), were the responsibilities assumed and carried by the children for order in the halls and rooms. Cleanliness as well as order was left partly in the hands of the students. Each class was responsible for keeping its own room neat and clean. Each day one or two students took on the task. In addition, halls and stairways were kept tidy by particular delegated classes. In a tour of inspection that took us into practically every room, laboratory and shop, we did not see a sign of litter— no untidy wastebaskets, not a shred or scrap of paper, dust or dirt on the floors of classrooms, halls or passageways.

In passing, we should note that the same neatness and order reigned in every public building, every street and public square of every Soviet city we visited. We were in the splendid new Leningrad subway at 5:30, during the evening rush hour. It was crowded with home-goers. We got off the train at one station after another. On the cars, on the station platforms, not a scrap of paper, not a cigarette butt did we see. Finally, on the floor of one station, in a corner, we found a scrap of paper as large as a playing card. To save the honor of the city, we picked up the paper and threw it in a nearby waste can. There are regulations against littering, but it is the people, not the regulations, that function. Each

35

Leningrad citizen is as proud of the subway as a father of his first-born. He would no more litter the subway floor, the art museum or the public library than he would litter his own livingroom. We heard the remark in a Leningrad street, "Comrade, don't be uncultured. Pick up that paper you dropped."

Some of our readers are sure to say, "You were on a guided tour. All this clean-up was to impress foreign visitors. When Catherine the Great went to take the air, she was driven through model streets and towns, decorated and refurbished and false-fronted to assure her that all was well and that her servitors were on the job. Her prime minister Potemkin saw to that. You were given the same preferred, prepared treatment."

We were on no guided tour. We made out our own day-by-day program, and sometimes changed it at the last minute, going to different places by different routes at different times. If Potemkin Villages were shown us, many thousands of Soviet citizens were busy day and night working to clean up buildings, streets, cities and villages all over the Soviet Union on the chance that two unimportant tourist visitors might come to town. It is absurd to imagine that the Russians spend their time thinking up ways to perpetrate hoaxes on foreigners. Soviet citizens welcome foreign guests. They show them around gladly and generously, but this is a small sideline to their primary activity of organizing and building up their own lives in their own country.

More than two million students are enrolled in technicums throughout the Soviet Union. Soviet technicums were established to fill a demand for education at the junior engineering level. They would be called trade schools in the West, and are designed to educate boys and girls who leave the ten year schools at 12 or 14 years of age to prepare themselves for some special field (such as transport, mining, mechanics) in which they wish to work. Those who leave the ten year school at the fifth year spend four years in the technicum. Those who leave at the seventh year spend two and a half years.

We looked through an oil technicum in Baku, one of the important centers of Soviet petroleum production. At the time of our visit, the technicum had 950 students in attendance and 250 correspondence students. The latter took examinations twice a year. Forty percent of the students were girls. Tuition was free. Students in the first two years of the course received stipends of 185 rubles per month, which took care of basic necessaries. In the third and fourth years the stipend amounted to 300 rubles. Students with excellent grades received stipends 25 percent over these figures.

We attended some of the classes. They were at the level of well-conducted engineering colleges in the West. The staff of 60 teachers all had high pedagogical qualifications. The building had 20 classrooms, with exceptionally good workshops and laboratory equipment. Much of the practical work of the students was done at oil plants or in producing fields.

"Do you have any trouble in getting students to attend this technicum?" we asked the director. He smiled. "We are filled to capacity. For each vacancy in the student body we have about five applicants."

Institutes offer, at the senior engineer level, educational opportunities similar to those that are provided by technicums at the junior level. Originally, specialized training at what we would call the college level was provided by Soviet universities. Universities included schools of medicine, engineering, teacher training, mining, forestry. Today the pattern has been altered. Each specialized field which seems to warrant the outlay in teaching personnel, buildings and equipment, is provided with one or more separate institutes.

Institutes have two chief functions: one is research, the other is teaching. In smaller communities the two functions are entrusted to one institute. In larger communities the two functions are likely to be separated. There are institutes which confine themselves largely to teaching. Other institutes, conducting no classes, take research students, and after the requirements are completed, grant them higher degrees. Still other institutes, staffed with specialists of the highest qualifications, do only research work.

We were in Tashkent, the capital of Uzbekistan. The Uzbek Republic has a population of some 8 millions. There are 31 higher educational institutions in the Republic, including two universities,—one in Tashkent and the other in Samarkand. In Tashkent there are institutes of agriculture, medicine, railway transport, machinery, electro-technics, irrigation and mechanization, finance and economics, law, the theatre, music and art.

In Irkutsk, in south-east Siberia, there are already many institutes for research and teaching. While we were there the Presidium of the Academy of Sciences of the USSR decided to set up nine new institutes in the Irkutsk district. Among them will be an East Siberian geological institute to study the most important deposits in Eastern Siberia; a geochemical institute to work out methods for surveying ore deposits in Siberia and the Far East; an institute of geography to study the natural resources of given districts with a view to the most advantageous sites for industrial establishments. Institutes of biology and metallurgy are also included in the plan.

Attendance is compulsory in the lower schools of the USSR. Those whose thirst for knowledge is still unslaked are urged to find a place (personally or by correspondence) in one or other of the institutes. From among these eager ones, by observation, by examination, by checking and re-checking, the abler and more talented are sorted out and accredited to the universities.

One of our young Soviet friends had graduated from an institute of foreign languages and had become an interpreter and translator. "I planned to be a geographer," she told us. "That meant getting a university degree. I presented my credentials to the Moscow University and took the examinations. In five subjects I got 'excellent,' the highest mark. In the other two I was marked only 'good.' That ended my dream of a geographer's career. It took six 'excellents' and one 'good' to enter that department of the university. I swallowed my pride and went to an institute."

"It must be a rugged job getting into a Soviet university. What proportion of the candidates who apply for admission in your school are accepted?" we asked the Dean of a Middle Asian university. "It varies with the department," he answered. "I should say the figure ranges from one-seventh to one-third." We put the same question at the University of Moscow. The answer was "One in ten." When a student graduates or drops out for any reason, nine others are competing to take the place.

Soviet students consider it an honor to be admitted to a university. Money cannot buy their way in. They must earn their right to a higher education through high scholarship and good conduct ratings. Once in, they must apply themselves in order to hold their position in the unceasing competition.

There were seven universities in Russia before the Revolution, few of them open to women. Today there are thirty-three universities in the USSR, open to both sexes. All the republics of the Union have their own universities, the largest being that in Moscow. There are 26,000 students in the

Moscow University, over half of them girls. Two thousand teachers head the twelve faculties in Moscow University: six in physical science (mathematics, biology, chemistry, geography and geology); and six in the arts (literature, history, philosophy, philology, law and political science).

Vyscheslav Yelutin, the Soviet Minister of Higher Education, in an article on "Training Scientists," wrote: "In that great area which is now the Belorussian, Lithuanian, Moldavian, Azerbaijan, Armenian, Kazakh, Uzbek, Turkmen, Tajik and Kirghiz Republics, there was not a single school of higher education in pre-revolutionary times. Today these republics alone have 152 universities and colleges, with 320,000 students enrolled. Of course, many additional thousands of students from these republics are enrolled in colleges all over the country." *

The Soviet Union has 34 medical schools (with 3 faculties, —in medicine, social hygiene and child welfare); 66 agricultural schools (with 7 faculties, in agriculture, chemical agriculture, plant selection, plant rearing, fruits and vegetables, agricultural economy, and mechanical agriculture); 19 veterinarian schools and 500 technical schools. There are correspondence schools for every subject. Three million men, women and young people are studying at correspondence schools or evening courses throughout the USSR.

Old Russia produced buildings like the Kremlin, Peter and Paul fortress, the Winter Palace and country estates for the powerful and the wealthy. Soviet Russia is producing schools, free education for everyone who is able and willing to learn, and countless institutions dedicated to culture. We found universities, institutes, libraries, museums, concert halls, opera houses, theatres prominent in every city. The

* USSR No. 2 (17), p. 4.

Soviet budget for 1958 calls for the expenditure of 212,768 million rubles for social and cultural undertakings.

When we entered Moscow in November, 1957, in the early evening, we drove into the city along a broad avenue which led from the airport through the Lenin Hills. Far off we saw a lighted tower shining through the mist. "What skyscraper is that?" we asked. "Our new university," they proudly answered. As we came closer, the Moscow University towered above us, ablaze with light, dominating the square miles of other lights which marked the presence of the city. Around the 425 acre university compound were springing up (in what were meadows a few years back) more clusters of buildings which will house the growing family of staff and students.

Here was a huge cultural institution covering every aspect of human achievement, its history, its present strivings and experiments, its hopes and plans for the future. Grown to adulthood in cities dominated by banks, office buildings, business houses and shops, we had often dreamed of communities in which things of the mind and the spirit would be recognized and acclaimed as man's most valued possessions. Well, here it was—a new world—providing for each citizen who was worthy, a chance to learn, to study, to attain and serve. As an earnest of good intentions, here was a university set above a rebuilt city, offering its rich cultural heritage for the illumination of Moscow, of the Soviet Union, of the world.

The educational ladder which we have been describing is not education for its own sake. It is a preparation for life. It offers the student a chance to learn, and it provides for the public services young women and men who have received special training for particular professions. People in the West take it for granted that an architect, a chemist or

41

a doctor should have special training. In the Soviet Union the same care is taken in the training of all those who serve their fellows, in any capacity.

This attitude was brought home to us in a Tashkent textile mill. During recent years the Uzbek Republic, of which Tashkent is the capital, has developed cotton-growing on a large scale. Abundant raw material and available power led to the establishment in Tashkent of a textile combine in which the cotton is turned into cloth. The mill employs 17,000 workers and staff members. Since we were in a remote part of Central Asia, our first question was "Where do you get your trained help? Such a large undertaking requires extensive expert personnel."

"That is no problem for us," replied the engineer who was showing us around the plant. "For workers who come to us with no previous experience we maintain a school in the factory. It offers a short course which acquaints beginners with textile production. At the moment there are 300 students in this factory textile school. Far more important than that," he went on, "are the regular schools maintained by the public educational authorities. At the lowest level is a textile technicum to which students go at 12 or 14 years of age, and where they spend from two to four years, advancing their general educational level, but with particular stress on textile production. From the technicum we get 16 and 18 year old workers who need not pass through our factory training school since they are already prepared to a large extent for their work here.

"Factory school and technicum provide us with beginners at the lower levels of skill and training," the engineer continued, "but a plant like ours cannot be run by slightly skilled workers. We require a large number of specialists in every department. These specialists get their training in our

Textile Institute which now has 2,000 students who have completed the ten year school or have passed the required examinations and who spend four years specializing in some branch of textile production. At the same time they are completing what you in the West would call an engineering college education. Graduates of the Textile Institute provide us with the trained personnel which constitutes the technical leadership in each department of our enterprise.

"This is not the last word, however," he said. "An enterprise must not only run well. It must develop new products and new processes and keep our plant equipped with up-to-the-minute machinery. To do this we must have scientists and engineers of the highest competence. These specialists come, in the main, not from our Textile Institute, but from our Institute of Polytechnics, which now has, 5,250 students, and our Middle Asian University, which has 4,000 students preparing themselves to be scientists and engineers at what you would call the Doctor of Philosophy level."

"Does this mean," we asked, "that an industry with 17,000 personnel does not go into what we in the West call the general labor market?"

He smiled. "The answer is 'No.' Our labor turnover is small. A few of our older workers retire each year; a few go into other occupations; most stay here. Our program of expansion calls for some additional personnel, but these come from the factory school, the technicum, the institute and the university."

Here was another angle on Soviet education. Its lowest round, the ten year school, trained everybody. Its upper rounds were reached by an able few. Throughout its length it was preparing citizens to take their places in a planned, ordered economy. Gone was the savage competitive struggle for jobs in a glutted labor-market jungle. The educational ladder prepared Soviet youth to climb into the places that gave them the best opportunity to make their contribution toward the building of a socialist society.

Soviet education is not a finished product. Educators are still theorizing and experimenting. At the 20th Congress of the Soviet Communist Party, Soviet educators were given a mandate to link theory more closely with practice. Pursuant to this mandate, large pilot projects have been launched to tie in educational institutions with economic and social processes. Students in the upper classes of ten year schools are to spend a part of each week in school doing academic work and the other part of the week in some segment of the productive process. This change is being made partly to familiarize students with work-a-day life and thus decrease the separation between head work and hand work, and partly to make it easier for students to pass from educational institutions into productive enterprises. Instead of spending sparetime on the street, students will be engaged in absorbing activities that will pay apprentice wages while they accustom young people to play an active part in the work of the world.

Students will be graded by the enterprise for the productive work which they have performed and will be examined by the educational authorities to determine the progress made by students in their work assignments. Soviet educators believe that such a program will necessitate an extension of the present ten year school to at least twelve years.

The experiment, involving fifty institutions of high school grade, is being conducted by the Pedagogical Institute of the Russian Federated Socialist Republic. Pupils in the last two or three years of the ten year school (at ages 16 to 18) will spend half time in school and half time in productive activity. For city schools this will mean three days a week, or alternate weeks, in school and in productive activities. (Soviet

44

schools function six days a week.) In the countryside pupils will spend the winter season in school and the open season on farms (half time at studies, half time at practice).

There is a strong movement in Soviet educational circles to have ten year school graduates spend a year or two at productive enterprises before they enter a higher educational institution. The coordination of academic and productive work during the last four or five years of a twelve year school would achieve this result without any sharp break between school and factory or factory and school.

The same Pedagogical Institute which is experimenting with school-and-job coordination in the upper grades of the ten year school is inaugurating a plan that calls for the building of some four hundred boarding schools in the Russian Republic alone. This experiment grows out of recent experience with boarding schools in remote Siberia and the far north, where winter travel is difficult. Boarding schools (or Internats, as they are called) have been set up in which pupils live through the school week, returning home only on weekends. Such schools have a double staff—pedagogical and housekeeping. Members of each staff are equally trained and qualified. Building costs of boarding schools for a given number of children are about three times the cost of ordinary schools. Maintenance costs are more than double. Parents who for some reason (either too many children, or sickness, or outside jobs) are not able to give their children adequate care at home can send them to these boarding schools for the school week. Children spend weekends and vacations at home.

We visited two Internats, one in Baku and one in Moscow. Both were pleasant, homey places where the children were in the company of other children 24 hours a day, instead of being a small unitary part of an adult world. They were taught by friendly teachers and mothered by warm-hearted housekeepers and nurses. They slept in decorated dormitories whose frilly curtains and bedcovers and little tables and cupboards had no institutional atmosphere. The children themselves were jolly and bright. They skipped and ran to their classes and gymnasiums and meals as though they were having a thoroughly good time. The house mothers said that they went home weekends with anticipation and returned to school at the beginning of the week with equal joy. The Internats we saw were successfully-functioning boarding schools.

Educationalists enjoy a fine school as a musician enjoys a fine composition or as a master mariner enjoys a fine vessel. During our 1957-58 trip to the Soviet Union we spent more time in schools than in any other Soviet institutions. First, because we value young people as the bone and sinew of the future society. Second, because we know more about schools than about any comparable subject. And third, because wherever we went in the Soviet Union there were young people who delighted us and schools which paid big dividends of satisfaction and information to anyone who invested time and energy in a visit.

One Soviet trade union official, who is also a fond parent, said to us, "The main thing is the thirst for knowledge that we have inculcated in our children. If they really want knowledge, the young people will find it,—of course with the help of us oldsters. If we can bring together a thirst for knowledge with a well-appointed means of supplying it, nothing else really matters. Youth, equipped with natural and social science, will find its own level and build its own world."

We have gone into some detail about an educational pattern that surprised and delighted us at almost every turn

by the great variety of opportunities which it offered to the
rising generation, by the patient thought which had gone into
its elaboration and by the initiative and imagination with
which educational problems were being tackled and resolved.
There is a very real sense in which the up-bringing of youth
lies at the core of Soviet life.

3. SIX MILLION EXPERTS

An expert is one who knows more correct answers to a
problem than the average person in a given situation. When
people are stumped, they go to the expert. Every time the
expert helps to solve a problem which has baffled others, his
or her reputation for expertness rises.

Traditional communities do not need experts. They follow the accepted way of life, make few innovations and meet
few new problems. Planners, organizers and administrators
whose day-to-day decisions control and guide productive processes or social institutions, depend upon experts. The newer
and more complicated the problem, the more indispensable
are the specialists.

Tsarist Russia got on with a tiny minority of experts. A
country composed chiefly of illiterate villagers followed tradition and abided by custom. Where organized trade and industry had developed, the limited number of Russian scientists,
engineers and technicians was supplemented by experts in
those fields, imported from Sweden, Germany and other
Western countries.

Disorganization during the War of 1914-17, the Revolution, and the ensuing civil war sent many of the foreign ex-

perts who had been working under Tsarism, back to their native lands. Russian skilled personnel was depleted by war losses and by defections following the revolutionary shifts of power. The result was a woeful lack of trained, experienced personnel in virtually every field of Soviet life.

Such shortages were doubly unfortunate since the new Soviet regime was not only committed to clear away war wreckage and restart the economic, political and social processes upon which urban life depends for its survival, but their aim was to replace the agrarian economy and social super-structure of Tsarism by a planned industrially based socialist society. Fulfillment of such a program depended at every turn upon the knowledge, experience, ingenuity, foresight and devotion of experts. Only a limited number of such experts could be secured from abroad. The vast majority had to be trained in the Soviet Union. Furthermore, their speedy training was a condition precedent to the building of a technologically advanced planned socialist society.

Training experts is a slow process. Human material (girls and boys, women and men) must be selected; schools and laboratories must be set up; teachers must be mobilized; courses of study mapped out. Educational institutions, properly organized, staffed and financed, could in the course of years turn out the needed scientists, engineers, technicians. But time was short, people were hungry and impatient, and the capitalist world of 1918 was scoffing, jeering, intervening.

It was from such inauspicious beginnings, forty years ago, that the planners and builders of the Soviet Union began preparing personnel for the monumental task of clearing away feudal-capitalist-imperialist wreckage and building socialism. The first task was to find, assemble and train the most human material.

Selection begins very early in the lives of Soviet children.

One of the first steps in the process is made at ages 8 to 10 when boys and girls have a choice between joining or not joining the Young Pioneers. All Pioneers are expected to spend some of their spare time in regular visits to Pioneer Houses, where they have a wide range of classes and groups under trained and experienced specialists. Child interest comes first and the Young Pioneer can go as far and as fast as he or she is able. The work of the children is carefully supervised. A girl or boy who shows aptitude or talent is urged to attend special classes or schools.

Special courses, classes and schools are maintained throughout the whole Soviet educational system. Pupils in elementary schools who show aptitude, for example, in music or in ballet, are advised to go to music or ballet classes or schools where, in addition to regular academic work, their specialty will be emphasized. Similar provisions are made for special work in other fields.

As the pupil moves from primary school to more advanced institutions, the same selective process is continued, with more specialization at higher age levels, until the student has graduated from a trade school, a college or a university and begun work in a chosen field. There he is still helped by his superiors. If he has ability or talent, at the end of three years of work he is advised to take graduate courses. If he agrees (and the oppportunity to do graduate work is a much-sought honor), the would-be graduate student, with a letter of recommendation from the director under whom he had done his practice work, takes his examinations. If he passes them he is given a monthly stipend and spends years in graduate courses, research laboratories and in related practical fields where his academic knowledge is put to the test of practical experience.

At each step in this selective process, from the early years of the elementary school, pupils are watched, encouraged, directed into the channels for which their talents seem to be best adapted.

Educational institutions are not alone in sifting out ability and talent. Shop foremen and directors of collective and state farms are on the look-out for talent. Factory classes and schools for young workers likewise are on the watch. Trade unions and collective farms are sending thousands of promising young people through educational institutions. If these students have dependents, special provisions are made for them. We visited one collective farm which had 120 of its young people away in higher educational institutions. Soviet society is on the search for special capacity, ability and talent at every level. At whatever age or in whatever department of Soviet life unusual capacity appears, it is given theoretical and practical scope for training and development.

"More than six million specialists—engineers and technicians, agronomists and veterinarians, teachers and physicians, artists and writers—are now employed in the country," writes Vyacheslav Yelyubin, Minister of Higher Education. "More than four million students are being trained in colleges, universities and specialized secondary schools. The number of persons with a higher education is constantly increasing. Before the war, 109,000 specialists were graduated from the colleges each year; in the past two years the number increased to 259,000 a year. This is the group which is mainly drawn upon for subsequent training of scientific personnel." *

Knowledge must be acquired before it can be accumulated. The source of knowledge is experience,—checked, classified, compared, verified. The general name for this process is experimentation, or more simply, research.

Research work has been carried on for centuries in many

* "Training Scientists," *USSR*, No. 2 (17), p. 8.

parts of the world. It is only recently, however, that research has been planned, organized and directed on a large scale. Today it occupies an important and honored area of Soviet life.

The RSFSR Academy of Pedagogical Sciences in Moscow is one of the Soviet institutions which has been set up purely for research. We were discussing educational experiments with the Vice-President. He listed some of the experimental schools that are being conducted under the direction of the Institute. One of them involves fifty middle schools; another 400 primary schools. "Our Institute has a staff of 550 specialists devoting full-time to research which is aimed at evaluating and improving various aspects of our educational system. Our work is housed in this central office, in seven special institutes in Moscow and one in Leningrad. Beside these special institutes we have two museums: one for public education and the other for toys. We have a special library of 880,000 volumes and a printing house. Our total staff is about 1200."

Similar institutes, dealing with the accumulation of knowledge in various special fields are housed in many parts of Moscow. They are to be found also in all of the chief population centers of the Soviet Union.

We met a group of students in a Siberian city with a population of about 400,000. "We have eight institutes which accept students," they told us, "including pedagogy, foreign languages, agriculture, mining, engineering, finance and economy, medicine and dentistry. Beside these eight teaching institutes, we have a number which do research work only, in medicine, biology, geology, chemistry and physics. Four other institutes are now being built and will be opened soon. They will deal with polytechnics, mining, rare metals and energy. We don't know whether they will be confined to research or will do both research and teaching." Here was

51

a provincial city in middle Siberia, with a score of specialized institutes, a good proportion of which engage only in research.

Knowledge, secured and classified, is filed in libraries. At every turn in the Soviet Union there is a library. Every institution, often every department of an institution, has its own library. The Soviet Union in 1957 had 400,000 libraries, including 147,000 public libraries, with a total of 1,500 million books and other items. In 1914 there was a library for 11,000 of the population. Now there is one for every 500 persons.

We were in the library of the Department of Geology in the University of Moscow. There were extensive shelves for books in regular use and a direct connection by automatic conveyor with the stacks of the central university library. There was a card index and magazine room, and general reading rooms in which every seat was filled. We also saw a special reading room for graduate students.

We admired the very full collection of current geological journals and periodicals. "We aim to get everything," the librarian said. "If we hear of anything new, we order it." We pointed out a journal from Holland, printed in Dutch. "Does anyone here read Dutch?" we asked. "Perhaps not among the students," said the librarian, "but we have faculty members and graduate students who cover a very wide field of reading. In any case, this and all other journals go to our digesting division. All of the articles and the important notes will be catalogued, digested, and translated if necessary. The digest will then be distributed to the Soviet institutes, departments, faculties and specialists working in this field." This well-staffed and equipped library took care of the needs of just one department of Moscow University.

The digesting system, to which the librarian referred,

covers about 10,000 periodicals in every department of human knowledge and in every language. Copies of these periodicals are processed in the digesting organization and in a phenomenally short period of time the digest is available for students, teachers and research workers all over the Soviet Union. Through this comprehensive service, Soviet specialists are kept in touch with the latest findings of their colleagues all around the world.

In Moscow there is a Library of Foreign Literature which collects material about foreign countries, in various languages. The Library, with a staff of 300, prepares, prints and publishes bibliographies of the literature published in foreign countries. We saw such a bibliography for Czechoslovakian publications. These bibliographies go to libraries and research centers all over the Soviet Union. The Library has two million items housed in two buildings. Its new building will be designed to house eight million items.

Heading the Soviet libraries is the fabulous Lenin Library in Moscow with its twenty million items, catalogued alphabetically and by subject matter. Seven million of these items are in 160 foreign languages. The library has twenty reading rooms with places for 3,500 and is open to all bona fida readers.

Topping this vast apparatus for the gathering, classifying and distributing information, are the academies of science. There is a Soviet Union Academy and there are local academies which serve the individual republics comprising the Soviet Union. These academies deal chiefly with the gathering, classifying and distribution of information for the Soviet Union, for the Republics and for individual cities which are directly responsible for education at various levels. In addition to this formal education there are numerous special educational activities conducted by specialized groups in every field of Soviet life.

A handbook on *Public Education in the USSR,* published in 1956, notes that "there are more than 5.5 million specialists with higher and secondary education employed in industry, construction, transport, agriculture and other spheres of economic and cultural development." The number of graduates from higher schools in the Soviet Union reached 258,000 in 1957. At present writing, the Soviet Union can send a hundred experts to India or a thousand to China as easily as the United States can send $100 million to Turkey or $500 million to Italy or France.

Needless to say, the provision of buildings, classrooms, laboratories, dormitories for the tens of millions who are attending Soviet educational institutions involves immense outlays by the public authorities. Such outlays are agreed to without serious question so long as their purpose is the advancement of knowledge and skills. Soviet institutions devote money and energy to training women and men who will be able to serve the Soviet public efficiently. In the United States there are several institutions such as Annapolis and West Point which train, lodge and board prospective experts for the armed forces. In the Soviet Union similar provisions are made for selecting and training experts in every department of Soviet life, peaceful as well as military.

4. STALINGRAD—CITY REBORN

Through forty years of pioneering the Soviet Union has lifted its citizens out of the black slough of illiteracy, instilled in them a thirst for knowledge, and gone a long way toward satisfying that thirst by making millions of them into trained and experienced scientists, engineers, technicians who can match wits and match products with the people from any other country. Today they are exercising a profound influence over the peoples and over many governments in Europe, Asia, Africa, and Latin America. In the course of this forty years, while the Soviet Union has provided leadership for progressive peoples across the world, it has re-organized, re-built and re-equipped whole areas lying within its borders and given the peoples new hope and a new life. It has also built new socialist cities, a phenomenon of the middle-twentieth century.

Stalingrad was the new name given to Tsaritzin, an old city lying along the Volga River in southern Russia. It had a population of 125,000 in 1925. Stalingrad entered the war, in June, 1941, a thriving community of 450,000 people. Two years later it was a heap of rubble in which there was not a single undamaged building left standing.

Invading German armies, totalling 330,000 men, attacked Stalingrad in their march toward the Urals. There was house-to-house fighting for months, with fierce battles fought back and forth on Cemetery Hill, the highest point of the city. There 15,000 Soviet soldiers were killed and buried, alongside countless enemy dead. After an occupation of the city lasting for 125 days, with Soviet defenders holding on in pockets along the Volga and being supplied by boats with ammunition and food during the bitter winter months, two Soviet armies drove in and cut the German lines. Ninety-one thousand German prisoners, including the top generals, were captured. Slowly the evacuated civilian population drifted back to the rubble-strewn area that had been their city. It was winter. Crowded into cellars, huddled in tents, they began the gigantic task of clearing away the wreckage and rebuilding their city.

Stalingrad by this time had become a world-renowned synonym for courageous resistance. Supplies and helpers came from Soviet areas which suffered less war damage. City planners and architects, from home and abroad, after surveying the desolation, advised moving the site of the city. "You have plenty of good building land along the Volga. Here are only tangled ruins. Select a rubble-free area. Begin over again."

The citizens of Stalingrad met, considered the suggestion, and rejected it. "We will rebuild our city on its old site," they decided. For a year they worked at disposing of the rubbish. Then they began to build, according to plan.

We saw this plan in the form of a huge, meticulously constructed model of the city-to-be. It covered many square yards of a large office in the City Architects' Building. We also saw the city, after fourteen years of resolute, determined, united effort. Both plan and fulfillment were monuments to human ingenuity, resourcefulness, and dogged persistence in the face of difficulties that seemed insuperable until they were tackled and surmounted.

We had a talk in late November, 1957, with the Vice-Mayor of Stalingrad, a tall and powerful woman who had stayed on in the city through the siege. "What are your impressions of our city?" she asked as we sat down with her in the Mayor's office. "Well," we answered, "this is the youngest city we have ever visited."

"Yes," she said, "we are only 14 years old. The second birth of Stalingrad began in February, 1943. Fortunately, it was a warm February. We were in total ruin. Three hundred civilians were in the city, with the soldiers. We had no houses to live in, let alone beds to sleep in. We built huts and lived in cellars, tents and wrecked planes and trucks that were lying about. In April and May, young Communists and other volunteers from all over the Soviet Union came here to help restore the city.

"Among our own citizens who returned in those early days was a well-loved teacher, Cherkasova, who immediately established a kindergarten and a school for those children we had with us. She organized a building brigade of women who worked with the men on the reconstruction of the city. These women undertook to rebuild the house of Sergeant Pavlov, a war hero. It was the first house restored after the war and it was done by this team of women.

"The brigade idea caught on. All citizens took a pledge to work, unpaid, in teams. They inaugurated "Cherkasov books" in which the hours they worked were entered. Some worked 500 hours for the restoration of the city. Some worked 1000 hours; they were the richest in honor. Since then, we have all worked at rebuilding. Now that it is almost done, it is still a matter of honor for us to continue working to beautify our city. We make parks, plant trees and shrubs and flowers, and tend and water them.

"Even schoolboys keep up their Cherkasov books. They collect trash and scrap, to keep the city clean. Every worker thinks it his sacred duty to work at beautifying the city. There is socialist competition among the brigades. This is the voluntary help that rebuilt Stalingrad."

Today Stalingrad is a splendid city of 700,000 people,—a population half again as large as that of 1941. It is a city reborn and rebuilt out of its own rubble and amid its own ashes. In the winter of 1957 we found the important tractor factory restored, enlarged and in full production. New factories had been built and were in operation. Of the war ruins practically nothing remained except the yawning walls and empty windows of a former factory that has been preserved in the center of the city as a memorial and a perpetual warning against the destructiveness of modern war. The city center has been rebuilt around broad faultlessly paved streets. Squares and fine parks let in sun and air and open wide vistas. Esplanades and a children's railroad skirt the Volga.

The students of the city decided they would build a Victory Park. They have been supplied with plans, specialists, engineering direction, and will work in their off-time on a huge culture park, with sport stadium, dramatic theatre, a concert hall, cinemas, rest houses, and a special section just for children.

An immense planting program is in operation. Flowers, shrubs and trees are to fill every available space. We saw four-year-old tree belts circling the city. With yearly rainfall of less than ten inches, the long hot dry summer makes it necessary to water every green thing planted, at least for the first few years. This the citizens have pledged themselves to do.

We were taken to a section of the city where streets were still rough and sidewalks not yet laid down. Here new building projects stretched in every direction. There were many small individual homes, self-built, by owners who borrowed up to 10,000 rubles from the city, interest free, to be repaid at the rate of 80 rubles per month. There were larger buildings, housing two or more families, constructed cooperatively

58

in spare-time by teams of home owners, assisted by organized groups of professional building workers. There were also big municipal housing projects in which the basic work had been done, including the installation of water, central heat and electric light. Inside finishing and decoration were being taken care of in spare time by the people who would occupy the new apartments.

We stood in one of these unfinished flats on a bitter winter day. The place was warm and the lights were on. The apartment we entered belonged to a young couple, recently married. Both worked in the nearby tractor plant. Both had ended their shifts and were busy with plastering and painting. The half dozen in our party, including a trade union official, an engineer, the Vice Mayor and a strapping jovial woman from the local peace committee, crowded its two rooms. All of them had been through the Battle of Stalingrad. All had been planning and working for fourteen years to re-establish their city. Now, with the results of their efforts visible on all sides, and with plan-fulfillment almost a reality, they rejoiced, relaxed, swapped stories and laughed together.

The object of their laughter, at the moment, was a story that had come over the radio. A woman visitor from the United States, prominent, highly connected, had been given the opportunity to go anywhere in the Soviet Union and see everything. After a month of travelling, she had recrossed the Atlantic and written in a newspaper article that she had never seen anyone laugh in Russia.

Standing on the littered floor of the unfinished apartment, the veterans of the grim Stalingrad battle repeated this story, holding their sides and shouting with laughter. The young couple stopped their work and listened with amusement. Never have we been in jollier company nor heard more spontaneous peals of laughter.

Another cheering, enlivening experience for us was a visit to a Stalingrad elementary (ten year) school. It was well-managed and well-equipped. The classrooms and halls, serviced by pupils under teacher direction, were orderly and neat. Classroom discipline (also teacher-pupil directed) was excellent. Pupils seemed to be deeply interested in their school work and determined to learn all they could. This school had 796 students and in 1957 graduated 94 pupils at ages averaging 17. Of the graduates, 68 entered institutes and universities to do advanced work.

The most unusual thing about this school was the teaching of English beginning in the second year, with pupils ten years of age. Ordinarily, the school director told us, the study of a secondary language began in the fifth school year, when the pupils were twelve. But after the war, so many parents in Stalingrad were paying to have their small children tutored privately in English that the school authorities decided to introduce English in the second year.

"Isn't it unusual for a single school to break away from the regular study course?" we asked the director. "Yes," he agreed, "but where there are social pressures and special demands, we try to meet them. We are going out of our way to provide the best education for our children. If parents feel that their children should learn English earlier, we will do our best to teach them. If the experiment proves successful, we may try English in the first year classes. We even contemplate running the whole school in English. With the children speaking English in school and Russian at home, they will become completely bi-lingual. If there is an equal interest in German as an alternative language, we will teach that earlier too."

"You study German here," we asked, surprised, "after your ordeal under the Nazis?" "Why not?" replied the director tolerantly. "Any cultured person should know foreign languages. German is one of the great languages of the world.

"The war had a profound effect on our people," he went on. "It made us more anti-war than anti-German. It also convinced us that if we are to get on together in this very complex world, we must know something about each other. One of the obstacles to communication between people is the language barrier. The learning of English and German will help in the understanding of our common problems."

We went through the school, stopping in various classrooms. In a third year class of ten year olds, one small girl volunteered to recite a verse in English called "Why, Willie, why, oh, why?" The "W" is hard for many Russians, because there is no corresponding letter in their language, but the youngster tackled the difficult couplet as though she intended to master it. Another small girl told about her cat: "My catch likes fitsch."

In a fourth year class we were greeted with "How do you do" and "We are glad to see you,"—from boys this time. Students in a fifth year class (12 years old) extemporized: "We live in Stalingrad." "Stalingrad is a large and beautiful city." "I am a Pioneer; I go to School Number Five." In an older group we came upon a teacher reading, in English, a science fiction story to the students. We argued with one young boy on the possibility of flying saucers being real and not imaginary. He defended fiercely the position that they were and could only be imaginary. However, he made friends at the end and said, "Please take our greetings and best wishes for peace and friendship to the children of America."

These children were courteous and friendly to strangers, if not quite at home with them. Among Soviet children we saw few bashful girls or boys. Most were upstanding, vocal and forthright.

61

While we were in Stalingrad, the young people were celebrating Youth Day. The evening rally was to be held in the auditorium of the newly completed Trade Union Headquarters which we were visiting. When we heard that the gathering was to be held that night we expressed interest and were cordially invited to attend.

Meeting time came and the balconied hall was filled with over five hundred young people. Before the entertainment part of the evening commenced, the local youth secretary spoke briefly about the world youth movement. "Youth in many parts of the world," said she, "do not have our opportunities. Either there are few institutions for higher education or else the fees demanded of students are so high as to exclude most of the daughters and sons of workers and peasants. The situation is different in the Soviet Union, where higher education is free and students receive stipends large enough to cover all their needs while studying. Since Soviet youth is so fortunate," said the girl, "it is our duty to do everything we can to assist young people in less fortunate countries. One way is the development of relations with youth of all countries in the interest of peace. We are happy to have with us tonight two workers for peace from the United States. We welcome them, and ask them to take back our good wishes to the young people of America."

A lad led off the program on his accordian with the Hymn of Democratic Youth, which all sang lustily. The evening was filled with their amateur performances. They sang, danced, played the accordian and mouth organ. In the intermission interval, as we strolled through the hallway, we were surrounded by avid groups of young people who questioned us keenly on everything from student's chances to study in the USA to the newest American plays, books and music. Each of us was the center of a circle, five or six persons deep, which only broke up reluctantly when the bell rang for the remainder of the performance.

Fourteen years have passed since Stalingrad lay in ruins. Then these young people now in schools and colleges were either babies or unborn. Their parents have reared a splendid planned socialist city for them to live and grow in. As we watched and listened during the few days that we were there, it seemed to us that the young people of Stalingrad are worthy of their heroic parents and of their shining new socialist city.

5. THE GREEN AND BLACK GOLD OF BAKU

Baku is located on the Caspian Sea, in the Republic of Azerbaijan, which is one of the fifteen republics composing the Union of Soviet Socialist Republics. A city of about a million inhabitants, Baku is in the midst of one of the world's oldest petroleum fields. Until eighty years ago, the petroleum (or "black gold," as they call it) oozed from the earth and was scooped up in crude dippers. In the 1870's British and other West European capitalists moved in with mechanized equipment and Baku became a boom town. At one end of the city were the oil millionaires, in their town mansions and on their country estates. At the other end lived the workers in huts and shacks that made Baku a hell-hole in an age of callous, ruthless exploitation.

Baku is long on oil but short on water. It is located on a receding salt sea, and surrounded by desert and semi-desert over which hot winds blow during the rainless summer. When Maxim Gorki visited the city, before the Revolution of 1917, Baku seems to have been at its worst—sprawling, gaunt, parched and, in the workers' quarters, squalid and poverty-ridden. Old inhabitants called the Shaumyan district of muddy alleys and broken-down hovels "the Black City." Gorki described it as the nearest thing to hell that he had ever seen, with dust and desolation everywhere and not a green leaf showing. One of us had been in Baku ten years after the Revolution. It was still a barren city in those days, but extensive improvements were being made.

After the Revolution of 1917 the people of Baku determined to make their Black City a Green City. First they increased their water supply. Then they re-planned their city and started rebuilding it. Finally they decided, despite the deficiency of rainfall, to make the city green. Year by year, this program was systematically carried out.

We were in Baku at the end of November, 1957. New buildings had sprung up everywhere,—individual homes, fine new apartment houses by the hundreds. Schools, hospitals, concert halls, administrative offices, institutes, libraries and other public buildings were new additions. Eight well-planned workers' settlements, with an abundance of green space, had been built in the Shaumyan District. Entire blocks of unsightly surrounding houses were pulled down and replaced by green-covered squares. Old and dirty canals were filled in and planted with flowers and shrubs. Rows of olive trees lined the streets. Property-holders covered each available meter of land with shrubbery and flowers. Tree-belts were planted at various points around the city.

We have been in many cities in the past decade. We think the greenest city we saw was Colombo, the capital of Ceylon. Its streets are lines of green and its open spaces are masses of rich, tropical foliage, with flowers everywhere. But Colombo is on an island, with two rainy seasons, during which it is deluged. The total yearly rainfall in Baku would hardly suffice to give Colombo one thorough tropical wetting.

When we went to Baku after their first snow of the winter, our comment was: "Baku is as green as Colombo." The planting had been so cleverly done, with such a mixture of evergreens and leaf-shedding shrubs and trees, that the city looked green even during the winter. Each young plant had to be staked against the high winds, tended and persistently watered, especially during the rainless May-September period. Yet so confident were the people of Baku in their future, that in the two years of 1956-57 some two million shrubs and trees had been planted, tended and watered.

The planting program for the next two years is even more ambitious. Its realization is made possible by a long canal and a recently completed artificial lake near the city. The lake will be thirty feet deep when it is filled. The water will be used only for irrigation and for industrial purposes. Baku's regular supply of excellent water comes from melting snows on mountains 150 miles away.

Baku is more than a green city. Its public edifices are impressive at every turn, from the splendid new Building of Ministries, on its imposing public square where rallies and celebrations are held, to the Nizami monument, park and museum honoring this 11th century poet and his successors. An elaborate memorial and park is dedicated to the twenty-six commissars of the post-revolutionary government who were seized by the British invaders in 1918 and shot early in 1919. The concert hall, the opera house, the Academy of Sciences, the new library, the pedagogical and other institutes are noteworthy for a city of a million inhabitants. Kirov Park is set high overlooking the harbor and the broad expanse of the city. The view from this vantage point, especially after dark, with the half-moon of twinkling city lights along the shore, reminded us of the beautiful curve of Bombay city and harbor from Malabar Hill.

65

One of our finest memories of Baku is of our visit to the University, which dates from the foundation of Soviet power. Before 1917 Azerbaijan had no higher education. Today, the Baku University has 5,000 students and a faculty of 400. There are eight departments: mathematics-physics; geology-geography; chemistry; biology; history, philology, law, oriental languages. Until 1929 the university had departments of medicine, economics and pedagogy. These subjects now are taught in three separate institutes. The university is conducted in the Azerbaijan language, with one section conducted in Russian. Seventy percent of the students are Azerbaijanians. Taught languages include English, German, French, Iranian and Turkish. The courses are generally for five years. In the four decades of its existence, the university has trained about 10,000 qualified specialists, who are doing important work in every phase of Azerbaijan life.

A reception committee of English-speaking Azerbaijan students welcomed us to the University of Baku. After meeting the officers of the university and members of the faculty, we were taken to an assembly hall where the students presented part of the program which had won first prize in the Youth Festival Contest staged in Moscow by the 15 republics of the Soviet Union. We were asked to give a short talk on education in the United States, after which a girl presented us with huge bouquets of local flowers and said in perfect English, "Allow us to congratulate you on your work for peace and brotherhood. We ask you when you return to your country to convey to your people what we are doing in the Soviet Union to build a peace-minded world."

Another memorable experience in Baku was our visit to the Oil Technicum which prepares qualified personnel for the oil and gas industry. Its students who leave the ten year schools after the seventh year, at age 14, spend four years in the technicum. Students who leave after eight, nine or ten years in the middle schools spend from two to three years in the technicum, which offers courses in theory which compare favorably with first and second year work in United States colleges. Their practice is done in the oil and gas plants and in the oil fields. A special technicum is conducted for the extraction of oil at sea. Founded in 1932, the Oil Technicum has graduated 5,000 students. Graduates in 1957 numbered 540.

Engineers for the oil and gas industry are trained in the Azerbaijan Industrial Institute, which has 5,000 full-time students and 2,000 correspondence students. Other institutes prepare engineers for transport, agriculture and the like.

Our last visit in Baku was paid to the Trade Union Council, which includes all of the trade unions in the city. The chairman of the Council, a woman engineer, briefed us on the changes made in the organization and function of the trade unions since the 20th Congress of the Communist Party. "Local and regional trade union councils," she said, "now have more authority and responsibility. They deal with matters of local concern at the local level, and are responsible for the use of their own funds. The Trade Union Council of the Azerbaijan Republic is practically autonomous.

"Thirty years ago," the chairman said, "Azerbaijan trade unions were in their infancy. Today they have grown to maturity and are exercising their responsibilities accordingly. Before the reorganization of the unions, there were many and wide discussions about it at the level of the trade union locals. The reorganization, which will be effected finally at the All-Soviet Trade Union Congress, had been carefully prepared in Azerbaijan. We are now carrying it into effect."

Azerbaijan and Baku are thriving, prosperous, going concerns, with their own industries, political leaders and educa-

67

tional institutions. They are going forward on their own power, as one autonomous part of the Soviet Union.

6. SOCIALIST TRIPLETS

After entering the Soviet Union we became accustomed to living among people who regarded socialism, peace and friendship as social norms, and who thought of capitalism, exploitation, imperialism and colonialism as monstrous aberrations. But we must confess to a feeling of real surprise when we found ourselves confronted with a socialist city which produced three socialist babies at the same time.

In the previous chapter we gave a picture of Baku's development as the capital city of a Republic and as a center of industrial, educational and cultural activities. We also stressed Baku's greenness. But we did not mention that its population has been growing rapidly to its present level of nearly a million.

Rapid population increase leads to crowding,—in housing, in traffic and many other aspects of city life. Crowding is something that Baku citizens view with alarm. Their city is now spacious. Most buildings are low. Streets, parks and other open spaces are more than generous. This makes for beauty. It also is pleasant during the long hot summer. But a city of a million people, built along such spacious lines, covers an immense area.

Population growth in Baku is no accident. It has paralleled the expanding demand for oil and its products, and for the development of enterprises designed to meet such demands. Oil production requires large quantities of metal piping and elaborate mechanical equipment for drilling, pumping and refining the natural oil. Oil industry equipment, needed in Baku, can be imported from some point in European Russia or the Ural mountains or it can be produced on the spot from the rich mineral deposits of Azerbaijan.

"We went over the problem carefully," one of our Baku friends told us, "then we made two decisions. The first was to produce our oil equipment locally. This involved building an iron and steel mill, a pipe mill, a machine-building plant capable of turning out oil pumping and refining equipment and also capable of building the heavy machines required to make pipe and the equipment for the oil industry. Such a project meant, first of all, an area sufficiently large to accommodate these extensive industrial plants. This requirement led us to our second decision. Since such industrial expansion could not take place without over-crowding and congesting the city we decided to locate the new plants beyond the city limits.

"After a survey, we chose a point on the shore of the Caspian Sea about 25 miles from Baku and went to work clearing up the desert and laying foundations for the necessary buildings. Desert it was, in truth," our friend continued, "with a rainfall of ten or twelve inches per year and hot south winds which parch the scorched earth all through a rainless summer. War came in 1941. For the next four years the high winds for which this region is famous piled the sand over the foundations of the new city. With war's end, the work began again. After the sand was cleared away, construction was started in earnest on City #1, Sumgait,—the name of the city-to-be."

When we visited Sumgait in November, 1957, it was a busy metropolis of 60,000. The big pipe plant, largely mechanized, was in full production and was being expanded. Near

69

it was a plant for building heavy machinery, including that required in a mechanized pipe mill. Much more, however, than new plants was required. Streets, housing, stores and recreational facilities had to be planned and built. When we were there, the streets were already broad and well-paved. A post office and city hall were completed, as was a hospital complex. Nurseries and kindergartens had been opened. There were ten year schools, a bakery, a restaurant, a lemonade plant, an ice plant, a stadium and a sport field. In the factories there were twenty dining rooms for workers. A hotel with two hundred rooms had been opened in the city. There were six concert halls, four culture centers, and a market for collective farmers. A technicum and polytechnical institute were being constructed.

Most of the building had been done since 1950. They had found stone nearby, of excellent quality. It was easily quarried and had been used extensively in constructing dwellings and public buildings. New apartment houses were well-designed and well-equipped, airy and open, situated so that as many windows as possible looked out over the Caspian Sea.

We walked down a broad residential avenue to the sea, where a beach and recreational facilities were being developed. On the shore we met two small girls playing in the sand. One was perhaps four or five, the other two years old. They spoke to us in a matter-of-course way, took our hands and walked us back toward the town, a touching gesture of friendship to complete strangers from two tiny inhabitants of the new socialist city.

While Sumgait was still an infant in years, and while there were still large capital outlays to be made before it reached the 100,000 mark in population, Sumgait was now a city in its own right, with its municipal government and its own budget. Baku's city Soviet, the Soviet of the Azerbaijan Republic, and the All-Union Government in Moscow had been generous in supplying funds and advancing credits. Thus the first of the socialist triplets had grown and prospered. Plans for further expansion were made in Sumgait, subject only to approval by the Government of Azerbaijan and the over-all supervision of the Central Planning Commission in Moscow. Sumgait was supplying many of the essential materials that made Azerbaijan one of the leading sources of the liquid black gold on which so much of the Soviet Union's economic activities depended for their fuels and lubricants.

Our Baku friend told us of the second of the new socialist cities. "Industrial plants require water. They also consume energy. Nearby rivers, which rise in the mountains of Iraq and Turkey, would supply both. A site was chosen near Sumgait for a dam which would furnish not only the water requirements of the new industrial city, but would provide water for irrigating a large acreage and electricity for the countryside."

Our friend paused. "If you will pardon a digression, the country folk outside of Baku were not only poor, but they lacked the simplest conveniences. Electric light for their villages was something about which they only dreamed. Still, they knew that in the early days of the Revolution Lenin had promised that every village in the Soviet Union would have electricity by 1970. So our villagers dreamed and hoped and waited. When the dam was completed and the generators were installed and light flashed across the Azerbaijan countryside, the villagers were overjoyed. "At last they have come," they cried. "Here are Lenin's lamps!"

"Our hydro-electric project at Mingechaur is the largest power station in the Caucasus region. Thanks to the dam, the collective farms get cheap electricity, water for irrigation and for watering the tree belts which should have a perma-

71

nent effect on our climate. Around the power station a new socialist city is developing, with its own industries and its own life. Already the population of this City #2 is 30,000. When we began planning for our steel mill and pipe plant we did not imagine that our search for water and power would lead to the establishment of two new socialist cities. But that is the way things have turned out. Mingechaur is still a baby, but already a city in size. It is a planned city and a by-product of a much larger plan."

Third of the socialist triplets is the city of Oil Rocks, 80 miles out in the Caspian Sea. Oil prospectors, checking over some reefs in the Caspian, found traces of petroleum. Plans were laid, an expedition was organized and a pilot well was drilled in 150 feet of water. It produced oil. More drillings increased the oil yield. It was evident that under the bed of the Caspian was an important oil field. Iron pipe, screwed together, was used for piling. Pile-drivers set the pipe in position. Platforms were built above high water level. Buildings rose on the platforms. Reefs and nearby small islands were used for extra foundations, and in the Caspian Sea, far out of sight of shore, grew the third socialist city, Oil Rocks, with its own housing, its culture center, its city soviet, its post office, theatres, hotels, restaurants, libraries, and its population of 15,000. When we were in Baku, this third socialist city was producing 30 percent of the petroleum of Azerbaijan.

All three of these socialist cities have grown toward adulthood since the war's end in 1945. Most of their development has taken place since 1950. There was nothing casual or haphazard about their birth and growth. All were designed to meet social needs. All were constructed according to plan.

Plans play a part in the life of every construction project. Factories, stores and dwelling houses are planned and built in any town or city in the private enterprise West, but with one important difference. In the West each building is a separate project, conceived and constructed according to personal whim and for personal advantage and profit, with little relation to other building projects or to the city's or society's needs. The socialist cities which we have been describing, and which are only three among many such cities that have been planned and built in the Soviet Union during the past three decades, were begun in answer to a socially-felt need and were designed and laid out with the general welfare as the first consideration. These three children of Baku, a proud socialist mother, have not been left to chance but have been conceived and born as an expression of human genius and in answer to the requirements of a growing socialist community.

7. TASHKENT AND ITS WHITE GOLD

Forty years ago much of Uzbekistan was semi-desert. The Uzbek people were more than 98 percent illiterate and the city of Tashkent was a collection of mud-walled huts, gathered around a trading center. Today prosperous collective farms stretch for miles across the former dry lands. Every Uzbek citizen born since 1910 can read and write. Thousands of them have become scientists, authors, teachers, engineers, doctors, actors, singers, technicians. Tashkent is one of the best-built, most prosperous centers of industry, education and culture in Central Asia. Three factors are responsible for this transformation,—the Revolution of 1917, water, and the white gold (cotton) which has made Uzbekistan rich.

Old Tashkent and new Tashkent face each other in the

mid-20th century. Mud houses, mud walls and muddy streets may be seen on the outskirts of the city, and even reach to broad avenues filled with motor traffic and citizens going purposefully about their business. On the other side of the avenue are the paved, tree-lined streets and the fine new buildings of the new city. Each year more mud buildings give place to present-day Tashkent architecture. The old city shrinks as the new city expands.

Since the current transformation of Uzbekistan is taking place as a result of changes in its agriculture, we begin by telling of a collective farm we visited in the open country, twenty miles from Tashkent.

"Forty years ago," we were told by the farm director, a small middle-aged man of ruddy countenance, "this land was owned by Uzbek landlords and Russian officials whose business it was to supervise the exploitation of the land workers. The land was unproductive chiefly because it lacked water. The land workers were poor beyond belief. How could it be otherwise? Rainfall here is irregular, from 10 to 25 inches per year in various districts, and is badly distributed through the seasons. Where cotton and other crops were planted, the seed was unselected, the soil was poorly tilled and fertilization was neglected. In the best years the crops were small. When rain failed there was next to nothing. After the landlords had taken their toll there was so little left that the workers and their families were fortunate if they could stay alive from harvest until the next planting. If you think I exaggerate," he added, "ask any man or woman here who is over fifty. They will confirm what I am saying.

"When we had harvests," he went on, "people lived in mud huts. When there was no rain and no crops, people lived in the streets. We were ignorant. Most of us had never even heard of electricity. Among the land workers, almost none

74

could read or write. Our fondest hope was to survive from one harvest to the next. The land has not changed. In fact, the land on which we are now standing was some of the poorest in this area. Much of it was waste land, producing nothing. It is we who have changed, we, and our way of life.

"For years after the Revolution we resisted change. We lived in darkness and feared the light. We worked hard with poor tools and poorer techniques. At the end of each year we had less than the year before. Our lives were hopeless. This collective was not organized until 1930, when the government gave us 1,520 hectares of land. Before the Revolution the land of this farm was mostly undrained and swampy in wet weather. It had to be drained and cleared for cultivation.

"Today our farm is laid out in this fashion: cotton, which is our main crop, 700 hectares, or nearly half the farm; animal fodder, 250 hectares; orchards and vineyards, 138 hectares; vegetables, 40 hectares. Our buildings occupy 120 hectares. The remainder of the land is in pasture. A small part is waste or bad land.

"A canal now runs through the farm. On it we have eight electric pumping stations. The entire farm is irrigated. We have 250 milking cows and 450 young stock and cattle which are being conditioned for market. We have 800 workers,— about half of them women. Before the Revolution only men worked outside. Women's place was in the home. Now men and women choose their work and are paid equally for performing the same tasks.

"A general meeting of the collective decides on the normal work-day in each department of work. Each worker or work team does a workday or norm of work and receives the regular wage. If a worker or a work team exceeds the norm, they are paid according to their product. On this collective, workers make from 600 or 800 to 3,000 rubles per month, depending on the nature of their work and the time they devote to it. No one is pushed. We take our own time and are paid in proportion to what we produce.

"Each family in the collective receives a tenth of a hectare (a quarter of an acre) of land on which to build a house. If the family desires it, the cooperative helps in the building. On this plot of land the householder may grow fruit or vegetables, keep animals or use the land as he pleases, so long as he does not interfere with his neighbors. The entire product of this piece of land belongs to the householder. The main crops from the collective fields are sold by the collective for cash. Rice, carrots, grapes (of which we grow 41 varieties), onions and other non-commercial crops are divided among the workers in proportion to work done.

"Members of the cooperative who are sick or incapacitated are cared for. We now have 120 on pensions which are provided by the collective.

"We have a seven-year school and a ten-year school. There are forty classrooms and 1,200 pupils. Ten of our teachers went through our schools, did their advanced work in higher institutions and have returned here to teach. We have three native languages here, Uzbek, Kazak and Russian. Besides these three, we teach English and German after the fifth year."

In answer to our questions about farm management, we were told, "Our procedures are entirely democratic. All affairs of the collective are decided in general meetings which are held monthly except in busy seasons, when they are held every two months. The general meeting elects a management committee, a director and an assistant director who serve for two years. The director must report three times each year to the general meeting.

76

"Gross income of the collective has risen from 8 to 14 million rubles during the last three years. This increase is due to the higher prices we get for our produce and to the greater quantity and variety of the goods we are marketing. With this increase in income we are reconstructing and expanding our buildings on a plan that will involve complete renovation of our farm by 1960."

Later, sitting at lunch with the director in his pleasant small home looking out over a gardened enclosure, we asked him about his own life. "I was born in 1909," he said. "We were very poor. No one in our family could read or write. My father was a good man. He always worked hard. His one ambition in life was to provide a decent living for his family. He never succeeded.

"I am a member of the post-revolution Uzbek generation. There is no illiteracy in our generation. I received my education in the Agricultural Institute in Tashkent. After that, I did three years of graduate work. Now I am a member of the Academy of Science of Agriculture. I have a regular job, a good home, a wife and five children. One is studying in the Institute of Biology, a second in the Engineering Institute, a third in the Institute of Economics. The other two are in our ten-year school.

"If my father had thought that I would be able to get an education, to find a steady job, to marry and to provide for my family, I believe he would have died of joy. In those dark days, such a life for the son of a peasant was to be found only in the land of dreams.

"Today such a life is enjoyed by millions of Uzbeks," he recounted glowingly. "We have two thousand collective farms, all are doing well. We have water and electric energy. This collective has running water in the farm buildings and in every house. The farm is completely electrified. Besides

77

our prosperous farms we have thriving cities with their educational, scientific and cultural institutions. We have a new life. With the aid of the Communist Party, following the thinking of Marx and Lenin, we have done these wonderful things in a single generation."

As the director of the collective talked with us we had watched appalled as his wife piled the table high with food enough for a week's eating. She brought on one after another carefully prepared Uzbekistan specialty, while all we wanted and needed was to sample the three or four different kinds of delicious grapes which were heaped up in the center of the table. The commiserating Westerners who sob over the "starving Russians" should have seen the table that day, or any of the other meals served us by Russian hosts. We said to her, "So much food! This is a feast!" "Oh, no," she assured us, "you would get this in any of our homes here."

Cotton, which is the main crop of this collective, stands first among Uzbek farm products, and Uzbekistan holds first place among the Republics of the Soviet Union for cotton output. Before the Revolution the Uzbeks raised about 500,000 tons of cotton per year. Now they are close to 3,-000,000 tons. (In 1957, a poor year, they told us, it was 2,750,000 tons.)

General plans for Soviet industry call for development along two lines: (1) getting manufacturing plants close to the raw materials; (2) building up undeveloped areas (which had existed on the margins of Tsarist Russia) to the highest industrial levels. In pursuance of these objectives, a modern textile combine has been established in Tashkent. Construction began on this plant in 1932. It was expanded in 1934, 1941 and 1946. In 1957 the plant turned out 400 million meters of finished cloth.

We have never seen a more modern textile plant. The

buildings were light and clean. The machinery was up-to-date and equipped with devices which protect against accidents. The workers were organized. One of the union leaders, with a woman member of the engineering staff, showed us through the plant. At the conclusion of our trip, in the packing room where bolts of finished printed cloth were being prepared for shipment, our guides showed us samples of their products and asked for criticism and suggestions.

"Twice a year," they said, "we show our new designs, invite consumers from the city and from neighboring collective farms and receive their suggestions. We are doing our best to turn out products which are good as well as useful, and which meet with the approval of our consuming public."

Beside converting raw cotton into marketable textiles, the Tashkent Textile Combine has built schools, hospitals and first aid units, clubs, culture corners, a maternity home, a nursery, kindergartens, sport organizations and a factory school for beginners. The combine is making special efforts to provide its workers with more satisfactory living quarters. Among the other industries which are developing in Tashkent is a factory to turn out the automatic machinery which a modern textile mill requires.

Before the Revolution, Uzbekistan did not have a single institution of higher education. In all of the schools there were only 17,000 pupils. In 1957 the schools were employing 70,000 teachers and providing for the needs of 1,300,000 pupils. Beside elementary schools, technicums, trade schools and special schools there were 31 higher educational establishments in the Republic, an Academy of Sciences, an Academy of Agricultural Sciences, a university, and a group of teaching and research institutes covering every important department of Uzbek life. At the beginning, professors and specialists were brought in from Moscow and Leningrad.

79

Now Uzbek educational institutions train their own personnel and are supplying specialists for other parts of Central Asia.

Tashkent has a Central Library, founded in 1870. Before the Revolution it was a small affair, with few readers. Today, with two million examplars on its shelves, its reading rooms are in constant use.

Before the Revolution there was one newspaper in the Uzbek language. Now there are 260.

Foreign languages are taught in a busy Institute with 1,150 full time and 800 correspondence students. Three students apply for each available place in the Institute. Nine years ago the Institute had 400 students. Today 500 are studying English, 420 German, and 250 French.

"Our Institute trains teachers, translators and interpreters," said the director. "Each year more foreign language is taught in our elementary schools. Our people are not satisfied with translators and interpreters. They want to speak and read for themselves. Each year more of our people are spending their vacations abroad, visiting, observing, studying. They are ashamed when they find themselves unable to talk to their foreign hosts. When they return they come to our Institute and say 'We must learn such and such languages.' They bring back books in foreign languages which they wish to read for themselves.

"If we are to build socialism," the director added, "it is necessary to maintain contacts and to establish friendship with peoples everywhere. So we are glad when people come to us, eager to learn. Such study provides the basis for culture exchanges, friendships and peace."

Our last evening in Tashkent was spent with the Rector of the University, the Secretary of the Uzbek Trade Unions and the manager of the local Intourist office. All had come from poor peasant homes. The Trade Union Secretary had been an illiterate orphan shepherd boy. He entered his first school in 1919 when he was eleven. The University Rector had begun his education after the Revolution. Today he is a famous mathematician, a member of the Uzbek Academy of Sciences.

"We men have gained enormously as a result of the Revolution," they told us, "but Uzbek women have gained much more. There is an Uzbek saying: 'It is better to give birth to a stone than to a girl. A stone is good for something. You can use it to build a wall. A girl child is good for nothing.' Today our young women are among our best students. They are employed in every profession. They do much of the work on collective farms and in factories, for the first time receiving salaries in cash and spending their money as they please. Women are school teachers, doctors, professors in our institutes, members of Parliament, members of the Uzbek Academy and Ministers of State.

"We had a revolution in 1917, when power was transferred from the landlords, officials and money lenders to the people. That was only a beginning. The changes that have taken place and are still taking place in our way of life are the real revolution, because they have opened up a future and given our people hope and confidence in the results of their own efforts to build a world of cooperation, peace and brotherhood."

8. THE SOVIET UNION OVER THE TOP

Beginning in early November, 1957, when we arrived in Moscow, we heard and read reports on "plan fulfillment." Soviet workers, management, State and Party officials had set production goals which they hoped to reach in the course of the year. As the year's end approached, they were casting up accounts, measuring successes, counting failures. Plan fulfillment was particularly important to them in this year because 1957 was the fortieth year since the Revolution of 1917.

Records were impressive. First came the figures for the Soviet Union as a whole. By comparison with 1913 (the last pre-war year under the Tsars) gross industrial output had increased 33 fold, while output of means of production had increased 74 fold. These increases had taken place despite the fact that almost half of the forty year period had been disorganized by invasions and wars and the mopping up operations which war always entails.

Since 1950 the national income of the Soviet Union had doubled. During the same period, retail prices had been reduced by about half. Within the last two years taxes had been lowered while pensions and the pay of the lowest categories of industrial and official workers had been increased. Payments to collective farmers had risen. Since the reorganization of agriculture in 1953 there had been large increases in grain and cotton production, in the numbers of animals on farms and in the output of vegetables, fruit, meat, milk and butter.

82

The facts can be put together thus: production has expanded in all sectors, but unevenly; investment has increased steeply; prices have fallen; the national budget shows a comfortable surplus; working conditions have improved; living standards have risen; necessaries and many comforts are in abundant supply; housing has improved in quality and increased in quantity; education has been made free; promotion is rapid; cultural opportunities are broadening. With such a stabilized, progressive economic base, we would expect to find a feeling of security and assurance in the present, and confidence in the future. That, in effect, is the story we heard on all sides.

In one instance we heard it in fluent English from a third year student of the Irkutsk Institute of Foreign languages whom we met in the airport, going to Moscow to join fifty other Soviet exchange students who were to spend six weeks in England,—four weeks in a university and the other two weeks travelling and sightseeing.

"Of course I am satisfied," he said in reply to our questions. "Why shouldn't I be? I began my education in a good ten year school in a Siberian village. Now I am studying in a fine institute under good teachers. Instead of paying for my education, I am being paid to learn. I get 300 rubles a month spending money. I am prosperous. When I graduate, a job will be waiting for me as teacher, translator, interpreter (whatever I like) with good pay, decent working hours and a chance for further study and for travel. When I find the right girl and she agrees, we will marry, raise a family, live comfortably, and help build up our country. What more could I ask?"

This case was typical of the confidence young people have in the future. Wherever we went in the Soviet Union the story was the same. Incomes were up. Prices were down. In every city the streets were thronged with well-dressed, energetic, cheery people. Stores were filled with goods and filled with buyers. There was no unemployment. Students had stipends. Cripples and old people received pensions. Everywhere young people were flocking into educational institutions to increase their skills.*

Behind this economic stability, security and progress lies a wide and increasingly planned control of both nature and society. Extensive geological and geographical surveys, reforestation, flood control, irrigation, the use of water for energy and transport, opening up of new mineral deposits and hitherto unused or little-used areas of fertile land, are coupled with economic and social planning and direction.

Examples are readily available. The 20th Congress of the Communist Party, in 1956, decided to decentralize political and economic controls by increasing the autonomy and authority of each of the fifteen republics which compose the Soviet Union. Decisions and budgets, formerly made in Moscow, are now made in the capitals of the republics. The economy also was decentralized and placed under the direction of local economic councils.

The trade unions, with their 49 million members (previously organized in 23 industrial unions with headquarters

* Some idea of the scale of Soviet economic advance is to be found in two brief sets of figures. The first was given by Secretary Khrushchev before the Ukranian Soviet on December 24, 1957. Total capital investments in million rubles: First Five Year Plan, 15,300; Second Five Year Plan, 29,500; (war intervened during the next five years); Fourth Five Year Plan, 67,700; Fifth Five Year Plan, 130,900; first year (1957) of Sixth Five Year Plan, 210,000. In each successive plan period, capital investments virtually doubled.

The second body of figures is taken from the Soviet 1958 budget (in million rubles): revenues from state-owned and cooperative enterprises, 570,314; expenditures for financing the economy—industry, transport, agriculture, 257,151; expenditures for social and cultural undertakings, 212,768. Income in the Soviet Union comes largely from earnings on the economy rather than from taxes. Very large sums are being spent for economic and social improvements.

in Moscow) were divided geographically into 160 regional and city trade union councils enjoying a large measure of autonomy, handling their own finances and electing representatives to an All Union Trade Union Congress which meets periodically in Moscow. Meanwhile the day-to-day business of the trade unions is transacted at local and regional levels.

Collective farms, which produce most of the food and agricultural raw materials consumed in the Soviet Union, were awarded higher prices for their products and were relieved to a considerable degree of tax burdens. A further step toward local autonomy was taken in 1958, when a decision was made to sell the machines owned by the 6,800 machine tractor stations to the collective farms, thus putting them in full possession of the equipment needed for their productive operations.

Speeches and declarations in November and December, 1957, after reports of plan fulfillment had come in, were jubilant. Said the Soviet spokesmen, "We have surpassed long ago the gross production of every capitalist country in Europe. Now it remains for us to excel in per capita industrial production and in per capita agricultural production. Within a measurable time, perhaps ten or fifteen years, we can expect to surpass the United States, first in per capita agricultural production and then in per capita industrial production."

Soviet leaders have determined to play a larger role in the non-capitalist world: first, by consistently opposing imperialism; second, by championing independence and self-determination for the colonial or semi-colonial peoples, and third, by rendering aid "without strings." This aid takes the form of technical help, of equipment, of loans at low interest rates, and of an extensive program of foreign delegations and individuals visiting the Soviet Union to study, to participate, or merely to observe and report back.

British, French, Dutch and Japanese imperialists have made loans and investments, rendered technical assistance, established trading connections, acquired control of natural resources, and have stayed in the colonies and dependencies until they were kicked out. With this horrible example of failure and disaster before them, Soviet policy-makers have been careful not to out-stay their welcome.

During the past eight years Soviet materials and machinery, Soviet loans and Soviet engineers and technicians rapidly boosted Chinese economy into a position where it could survive and advance under its own momentum. Today Soviet personnel has withdrawn or is withdrawing from the Chinese People's Republic. Materials, machines and personnel in all fields of the economy were largely Chinese by the end of 1957.

Soviet experts are directing the building of a million ton steel mill in India. When it is completed, the Indians have every reason to believe that it will be their mill, with neither dictation nor interference from the Soviet Union.

One does not have to travel far in Europe, Asia or Africa to realize that the Soviet Union is out in front and ace-high with those peoples. A Moscow dance team volunteered to visit Cairo early in 1957 to help raise funds for the Suez invasion victims. It was rapturously received. The Soviet Antarctic ship "Ob" went to Genoa in October, 1957, at the time of the Columbus Day celebrations. The crew and officers got an official welcome and were given the freedom of the city. It did not take these visits or the five million-strong crowds lining Khrushchev's and Bulganin's way into Calcutta in 1956 to demonstrate the extent and the depth of pro-Soviet feeling in these areas.

Cultural exchange is one of the most important means used to acquaint foreigners with the Soviet Union, and Soviet citizens with the outside world. Cultural exchange takes many forms,—the exchange of information, of art objects, of scientific achievements, of teachers and students, of delegations representing different aspects of life. During 1957 the Soviet trade unions acted as hosts to 355 delegations of foreign workers from 80 countries, including 68 capitalist countries. These 355 delegations were made up of 2,800 individuals. Reciprocally, 1700 Soviet Trade Unionists went abroad. During 1956, from China alone, 95 delegations representing various interests visited the Soviet Union, while 87 Soviet delegations visited People's China.

Historical events have their reasons. Tempestuous advances like those made in the Soviet Union during the first forty years of its existence are no exception. Objectively the upsurge of the Soviet Union since 1917 is one part of an explosive transformation that is hustling capitalist imperialism off the stage of history and, in its place, ushering in a rational, planned, orderly, socialist pattern. Subjectively, the upsurge in the Soviet Union has been anticipated, directed and guided by the Communist Party and its two associates,—the Young Communist League and the Young Pioneers.

Several assumptions underlie the work of the Soviet Communist Party. (1) In a society of industrial workers, land workers and intellectuals, there are no special privileges. All groups are equal. (2) Some individuals and groups in such a society are more active and experienced than others. The most active and experienced compose the advance guard. (3) Advance guard elements are not apart from the masses, but a segment of the masses. Only as they preserve and enlarge their mass contacts can they hope to lead. (4) Advance guard elements in the Soviet Union compose the Communist Party and its allies and associates, the Young Communists and Pioneers. They can provide effective leadership only so long as they maintain close contact with the masses, or as Lenin put it, "together with the masses and ahead." (5) Communist Party members, who come from all groups, have as their main purpose to develop consciousness among the masses and loyalty to the Party, so that they will say: "The Communist Party is our party." (6) One of the chief tasks of the Party is to bring up the young in full consciousness of their responsibilities before the people.

The Communist Party is the only legal party in the Soviet Union. In this respect it differs from Western countries in which Communist parties are, without exception, minority parties with no general mandate to make and implement public policy. In the Soviet Union, on the other hand, public policy is determined by the Communist Party, ratified by the government and presented to the electorate in a way that presumably will win their support. If the Communist Party assumptions printed in the previous paragraph turn out to be valid, the Soviet Union will survive and prosper, because the Communist Party is giving it effective leadership and therefore winning and holding public support and approval.

The Communist Party in the Soviet Union has on its membership rolls only a small proportion of the total population. At the close of 1957, membership figures for the various Communist organizations were: the Party, 7 million members; the Young Communists, 18 million members, the Young Pioneers, 18 million members. Party members, Young Communists and Pioneers together make up only 22 percent of the total population of the Soviet Union. It is a minority, not a majority party. In this fact, argue the Communists, lies

88

the Party's strength. It consists of the militant, vocal, qualified minority.

Party members, particularly younger ones, do much of their work among the Young Communists. Young Communists do much of their work among the Pioneers. All three organizations derive their strength from the people and are dedicated to the service of the people. Each organization is autonomous. All serve the same general purpose.

Membership in all three organizations is voluntary. No one is forced to join. What the Party wants is enthusiastic volunteers. It has no place for conscripts.

The Party works in close association with the peoples' organization,—the trade unions, the collective farms, the women's and sports organizations, the educational, scientific and cultural institutions, and with the agencies of government. In the Soviet Union, the treasures, land, industries, utilities, institutions, all are in the hands of the people. It is the aim of the Communists to make the people aware of their trust and faithful in preserving and developing their invaluable possessions. The Party does not work out policy and force it on the people. It expresses the popular will and leads in the effort to put the popular will into effect. Many Party meetings are widely and openly held and attended by non-Party elements. The Party is criticised and invites criticism in private and in public. The people trust the Party because of its long record of service.

Here, again, is something new under the sun. In political structure as in economic organizations, the Soviet Union differs in many essential particulars from Western countries. The Brave New World is not merely brave and new; it is also different.

PART TWO

"Men of righteousness! Good health to you! Continue your struggle for justice! The future is bright! That brightness is beckoning to you! It is for us to exert our efforts and fight for it!"

Letter of Wang Hsiao-ho to his fellow prisoners before being put to death September 25, 1948, by the Kuomintang, for his revolutionary activities in the Chinese Communist Party and the Shanghai Electrical Trade Union.

1. THE CHINESE PEOPLE WIN

China's people were burdened with wars, local and national, for a century. Beginning with the First Opium War in 1840 China was invaded, exploited and occupied by foreign imperialists. Chinese ports were opened forcibly to western merchants and traders. Opium was imported from India and sold in Chinese markets despite anti-opium laws and protests from the Chinese government.

The Opium War resulted not only in the utter defeat of the Chinese armed forces and the whittling away of Chinese sovereignty, but in the levying of indemnities, the increase of taxes and the worsening of Chinese living conditions, all of which led to a series of armed revolts and culminated in the Taiping Revolution of 1851-64. The Taipings fought their way from the interior of the country and established a government in Nanking in 1853. They took the land from the landlords, distributed it among the peasants, provided that the army should be loyal to the people, adopted a liberal trade policy, reduced taxes, banned the opium trade, outlawed gambling and corruption, granted women legal and economic equality with men, abolished prostitution and the sale of women, and opened civil service examinations to women as well as men.

Alarmed by these progressive measures, imperialists with vested interests in China went to the assistance of the Manchu Monarchy. Nanking, the Taiping capital, was captured in 1864, putting an official end to the revolt. But war losses had been so heavy that the monarchy was never able to re-establish its hold over the Chinese people.

Japanese armed forces defeated the Chinese in the War of 1894-95. Under the treaty of 1895 the Japanese Government secured control of Taiwan and the Penghu Islands, gained a foothold in Korea, won the right of Japanese business interests to set up industries in China, opened new ports and levied a heavy war indemnity. Seeing the weakness of the Manchu regime, Britain, France and Russia demanded additional concessions from China. These new humiliations led to widespread unrest which crystallized in the Boxer movement of 1899-1900. Again the imperialists intervened, invaded China, captured Peking and levied a heavy indemnity against the Chinese. Unrest increased. Revolutionary forces overthrew the ineffective Manchu regime in 1911. A Republic was proclaimed in 1912 with Dr. Sun Yat-Sen as its first President. The hold of the revolutionaries was weak and the local warlords were strong. For years rival cliques struggled for power, with the imperialists backing one warlord against another. In 1921, with the formation of the Chinese Communist Party, the oppressed workers and peasants found leadership for their epic struggle. The revolutionary armies from the south came very near to establishing themselves in Central China in 1926. Their plans were shattered when Chiang Kai-shek, the commander of the revolutionary forces, turned on his left-wing comrades and allied himself with the landlords, merchants, warlords and imperialists.

For the next ten years, Chiang (with the support of the "Four Families of China" representing the bankers and money-lenders, the landlords, the commercial and industrial capitalists, in close alliance with the imperialists) conducted a series of savage extermination campaigns directed against the left-wing liberation forces. The Chinese people suffered from banditry, the struggles between warlords, the civil war between Chiang and the Chinese Communists, and the international war fought in the main between the Chinese Communist forces and the invading Japanese. The Japanese were defeated in 1945. Three years later, in 1948, Chiang's forces were driven from the Asian mainland. In 1949 the Chinese Peoples' Republic was proclaimed.

Imperial intervention and invasion, civil war and two major international wars had disturbed the peace and well-being of the Chinese people from 1840 to 1948. Excessive taxation, inflations, boycotts, blockades and the destruction of battle had disorganized the lives of millions and caused countless wounds and untimely deaths. Liberation brought an end to this century of disunity, discord, conflict and needless suffering. It also brought an end to the century of humiliation that began with the First Opium War in 1840.*

Every question that we asked as we travelled around China in the early winter of 1957-58 drew an answer containing these words: "Before Liberation matters stood thus and so. Since Liberation such and such changes have occurred." So universal were these phrases that in our notes we began writing "BL" for Before Liberation and "AL" for After Liberation.

"Liberation" has the same meaning for the Chinese people that "emancipation" had for the Negroes of the American South. It does not refer to a particular date, but to a change in status. The Republic was officially proclaimed on October 1, 1949. For years before that day, however, areas of China were "liberated" from landlordism, extortion, usury, from the exactions of Chiang's armed forces, from helpless poverty and hopeless ignorance.

---

* Anyone wishing to understand living conditions in pre-Liberation China and the long and bitter struggle which preceded Liberation should read a first-hand account by a participant. *The Great Road,* The Life and Times of Chu Teh, by Agnes Smedley, N.Y.: Monthly Review Press, 1956.

Liberation marked a tremendous change, not only in the internal life of China, but in China's international position. For a century the Chinese government and people had been pawns in the game of power politics and victims of imperialism's insensate greed and unbounded power-hunger. On the day of Liberation the Chinese people "stood up" and overthrew their domestic oppressors and exploiters. They also brought to an end the century of defeat and dishonor which had begun in 1840 with the First Opium War.

Millions of overseas Chinese have gained in self-respect because of the economic, political and social restoration and construction that followed Liberation. Travelling through south-east Asia in the winter of 1956-57 we met Chinese intellectuals, businessmen and professionals. Whenever they spoke of People's China it was with respect and a fierce pride. "We may not be Communists," some of them said, "but we are Chinese. For a hundred years our motherland was the prey of imperialist vultures. Now that China has taken its rightful place among the great powers, we Chinese can hold up our heads once again and look our fellow men in the face."

Liberation did not bring immediate peace to China. On Taiwan Island, on Quemoy and Matsu islands, Chiang kept an army of half a million,—trained, financed and supplied by the United States Government. American ships and planes, based on Okinawa, the Philippines and Japan, were on China's doorstep. Washington's policy toward China's new regime hardened. A year after Liberation, United States armed forces were on the march to the Yalu River and toward China's North East territories. Nearly three years of battle and negotiation were to pass before the Chinese people and their new-born Republic were able to launch their First Five Year Plan, in 1953, and begin to practice the arts of peace, self-determination and socialist construction. The Korean War marked a turning point in the history of the Chinese people who had endured a century of international and civil strife, major invasions by foreign powers, ruthless oppression and merciless exploitation in their homeland. With the armistice in Korea and the inauguration of the First Five Year Plan, the Chinese people began a new epoch of independence, self-determination and the planned, ordered development of their resources and their lives.

Chinese economy had passed through a century of disturbance and disorder. Each invasion, each war, each revolutionary upsurge had disorganized agriculture, upset trade, raised taxes, led to price inflation, and, in some cases, to currency devaluation. Immediately after Liberation Chinese economy faced the task of mopping up the past, of modernizing and industrializing. Economic reorganization called for materials, equipment, capital and skilled personnel. The need was met from three directions. First, there was an economy or austerity movement that swept across the country and gained wide support; second, there was a Five Year Plan for economic and social development; third, there was help from abroad.

China's economy movement, in its simplest form, was an effort to live frugally and economically, to achieve maximum productivity with minimum expenditures and to invest savings in new capital equipment. "By integrating the virtue of frugality into our whole national life," wrote Chen Hanseng in *China Reconstructs* *, "we hope to lighten the burden of financing China's socialist industrialization." The economy movement went far beyond "saving" in the classical sense of that term. It aimed at reducing outlay while maintaining income. It also aimed at keeping the supply and the

* October, 1957, p. 25.

marketing of commodities in balance. Furthermore it was designed to lay aside each year a reserve against contingencies and emergencies that might arise in the following year.

Such sentiments are far removed from the current Western practice of deficit spending, or buy-today-pay-tomorrow. They are a restatement of the simple economic principle of keeping outgo inside income and thus creating a margin which can be used for improvements and betterments.

In pursuance of this policy, the budget was kept in balance. Salaries and wages were raised only after increases in productivity. Top priority was given to heavy industry, but light industry was expanded fast enough to keep pace with the purchasing power of the growing wages fund, which was being augmented by the movement of men and women from agriculture into industry, transportation and construction, and the payment of cash income to members of agricultural collectives. Thus equilibrium was maintained within the economy as a whole.

Symbolizing this entire movement for economy was uniformity in clothing. In place of a great variety in color and cut, the Chinese people, male and female, wore blue trousers, shirts and blue jackets buttoned tight at the neck. In the North, in winter, heavy warm underclothes were added; trousers and jackets were padded, and overcoats were sometimes worn. There were some differences in the quality of cloth, but as a whole the population was dressed the same. The purpose of this uniformity was to economize on styling, dye and material. The padded clothing also saved on fuel, because the Chinese, like the Japanese, tend to "heat the body not the room." They do not have central heating in many of their houses, shops or theatres.

Money savings from clothing uniformity were considerable over the years. The real gain, however, was in the sense of brotherhood and equality which the uniformity produced. Chairman and premier, managers, skilled craftsmen, unskilled workers and farmers, men and women, all were dressed the same. They were all Chinese, dedicating their lives to the building of socialism and not bothering too much about outer appearances. The villagers have a saying: "First rags, then patches, now whole clothes." China is in a state of "whole clothes," with evidences, in the winter of 1957, of increasing variety, color and cut of clothing on display in the stores and worn on the streets.

Waste was an evil New China would not tolerate. Economy was to be practised nationally and individually. Land, money, cloth, food, water, electric power, all were to be used with the greatest care. Extravagance and ostentation in any form were excoriated. Those who wasted food or materials were enemies of society and were admonished, if not punished.

Another item was carefully watched: the ratio of spending power in countryside and city. "Under the old regime," wrote Chen Han-seng,* "the countryside was exploited by the city. Large sections of the peasantry were taxed and surtaxed into destitution." Builders of socialism are placing the chief tax burden where it belongs, on industry and the city population. To correct the old unbalance, the purchasing power of the Chinese countryside has been increased more rapidly than that of the city.

The economy movement emphasized care and discrimination in outlay. Planning stressed higher output. China's 650 millions had lived meagerly, and many of them wretchedly, before Liberation. If they were to enjoy the decencies and amenities of life they had to raise efficiency and the total volume and variety of products. Such a result could be

* *Ibid.*, p. 24.

brought about most speedily and surely by scientifically-based social planning.

The general purposes and prospects of planning are laid down in the Preamble to the Chinese Constitution of 1954: "The system of people's democracy—new democracy—of the People's Republic of China guarantees that China can in a peaceful way banish exploitation and poverty and build a prosperous and happy socialist society. From the founding of the People's Republic of China to the attainment of a socialist society is a period of transition. During the transition the fundamental task of the state is, step by step, to bring about the socialist industrialization of the country and, step by step, to accomplish the socialist transformation of agriculture, handicrafts and capitalist industry and commerce."

People's China in 1952 published an over-all plan for social improvement. The plan aimed at industrializing an agrarian economy, based chiefly on handicraft and seriously deficient in transportation and means of communication. It covered five years, from the beginning of 1953 to the end of 1957. We do not intend to discuss the Chinese economy or to go into the details of the First Five Year Plan. Solomon Adler has covered this field in his excellent book, *The Chinese Economy*.*

The general purposes of the First Five Year Plan are summarized thus in the *Handbook on People's China* **: "To lay the groundwork for socialist industrialization and for the socialist transformation of private industry and commerce."

The Second Five Year Plan, begun January 11, 1958, aims "to continue industrial construction with heavy industry as its core and promote technical reconstruction of the

* N.Y.: Monthly Review Press, 1957.
** Peking: Foreign Language Press, April, 1957, p. 101.

national economy, and build a solid foundation for socialist industrialization, to carry through socialist transformation, and . . . to reinforce the national defense and raise the level of the people's material and cultural life." *

People's China's approach to the problem of conscious, planned, social improvement may be summed up in their phrase "step by step". It has taken more than four thousand years to bring Chinese society to its present level of development. They cannot transform the country over-night. The Communist Party initiated the Five Year Plan. The organs of state authority, including the State Planning Commission, approved it, put it into effect and guided it to successful fulfillment. The plan included projects involving flood control, power development, the building of heavy and light industry, railroads and highways, irrigation, and the transformation of a private enterprise economy, step by step, into a socialist economy.

China's First Five Year Plan involved unusually heavy government spending: 132,210 million yuan from 1953 to 1957 inclusive. Half of this amount (48.7 percent) was devoted to economic construction; 14.7 percent to education, culture and social services; 31.1 percent to national defense; 5.5 percent to repayment of loans. During these five years almost two-thirds of the nation's expenditures were devoted to economic and cultural advancement.

Sources of revenue changed somewhat during the five years of the plan. In the first year, 63 percent came from socialist state enterprises; 17 percent from private capitalist enterprises, and 13 percent from the peasants. In the fifth year, socialist state enterprises provided 72 percent of the revenue; private enterprise 1 percent, and the peasants 11

* *Ibid.,* 112.

percent. These figures suggest a steady trend toward socialism.

Stability in the economy produced stability in prices. Both the wholesale and retail price index moved up slightly, causing a small increase in the cost of living. Against this, there was considerable rise in the money incomes of workers (especially the lowest paid) and farmers. The result was a feeling of confidence and security that was shared by the great majority of Chinese in 1957. The economy was stable, production increased, the incomes of workers and collective farmers were raised at the same time that hundreds of factories, bridges, schools, dwelling houses, culture centers and rest homes were completed. Doubters were invited to inspect the factories and schools and to cross the bridges.

How many times, during the century of conflict that preceded Liberation had the Chinese people been promised a better life! How often had they sacrified, struggled and died in their efforts to win freedom from oppression! Time after time the victory seemed within their grasp, but backwardness and oppression regained the upper hand.

Liberation came in 1949. The Chinese people stood up. After Liberation they spent years clearing up the debris, restoring life to a level of pre-war normalcy and stabilizing the economy and the society. With routine tasks out of the way, they were able to give serious attention to building socialism. For a decade they have had a chance to sample the life of responsible planning, building and organizing through which alone a whole people can hope to enjoy the better things of life.

Final hurdles must be crossed before the Chinese people can hope for a full life of peace and happiness. Foreign armed forces must be removed from Chinese territory and from adjacent island bases. Remaining counter-revolutionary elements within the country must be dealt with. The threat of foreign espionage, subversion and armed invasion must be eliminated. It is not enough to establish reason and justice in one country. Before the task is finished, the entire human family must rationalize its economy and organize its life to promote the general welfare.

With Liberation the Chinese people won independence, unity and self-determination, the possibility of drawing up their own plans and going their own socialist way toward order, conservation, literacy, better health, cooperation, shared responsibility for the general welfare, justice, peace and brotherhood. After a century of economic, political and social upset and turmoil, the Chinese people have enjoyed five years (1953-58) of stability and security based on planned, orderly, progressive advance to higher levels of individual and community well-being.

2. CHINA'S GOOD EARTH

China's land area is 3,860,000 square miles, or a quarter greater than the area of the United States. Over 90 percent of the country is in the north temperate zone. South China is sub-tropical. Two-thirds of China is mountainous. On much of the remaining third, rice and cotton can be successfully grown.

During our travels around the world we do not remember seeing better earth nor more careful cultivation and utilization of the soil. Never have we seen stretches of such fertile land, much of which, after producing crops for centuries, is probably at least as productive today as when first cultivated. Chinese people tend their land and conserve it with

103

ceaseless loving care. On no other basis could they support the present population of 650 millions.

Nature is not always friendly. In China as elsewhere there are floods and droughts. Such disasters are made more destructive by the absence of forests. It is possible to travel for miles even in the most fertile parts of China without seeing any grouping of trees that could be called a forest. No one seems to know when the Chinese hills were denuded. Soil and climatic conditions would lead one to assume that at some time they were covered with trees. Mountainous areas in the more remote parts of China still are heavily forested.

Since there is no forest floor to hold water on many of China's hills and mountains, falling rain and melting snow rush in torrents down the bare hillsides and into the streams and rivers. The result is waterless hills and flooded valleys. The concentration of rainfall in the summer months increases the probability of soaked earth, quick run-off, flash floods for part of the year and water shortage for another part. Flood danger is increased by the steep gradient of Chinese rivers, which flow rapidly from some of the world's highest mountains toward the plains and the sea.

Rivers like the Yellow, the Min, the Huai and the Yangtse have been flooding periodically for centuries. The Yellow River, second longest in China, is known as "China's sorrow" because in the last three thousand years the river has broken out of its banks about 1,500 times. On 26 occasions it has changed its bed in the lower reaches, causing great loss of life and property.

Efforts to control the turbulent Chinese rivers began many centuries ago. About 250 BC, a brilliant governor and engineer named Li Ping built a diversion dam and a series of canals in an attempt to control the Min River. The project included two major canals, 620 distribution canals and 2,200 irrigation ditches with a total length of 724 miles. The project irrigated half a million acres. Practically all of the construction work was done by hand. Parts of this canal system, begun more than 2,000 years ago, still are being used. After 1949 the system was repaired and greatly enlarged. Despite these and many similar efforts, alternating flood and drought have continued to play havoc with China's agriculture down to the present day.

Flood control, hydro-electric power development and irrigation were given top priority immediately after Liberation. One of China's most intractable and destructive rivers, the Huai, was scheduled for control by 1957. Much of the work on this river was completed by 1956 and the heavy floods of 1957 did a minimum of damage. Extensive projects are now under way on the Yangtse, the Yellow and other rivers. The 46 dams scheduled for the Yellow River will not be completed until about 1975. When this "staircase project" is finished, the Yellow River should be flood-free and its waters should be so completely under control that they can be used for productive purposes.

Since Liberation the People's Government, while planning eventual river control, has handled each flood situation as it arose with vigor and determination. During the summer of 1957 in North West China, one rainy spell lasted for 28 days. The result was a record flood level. Before Liberation the entire district would have been heavily innundated, with immense losses of property, livestock and human life. But 1957 was different. River dikes had been raised and strengthened and materials had been gathered and stockpiled to take care of normal flood waters, but this was no normal flood. Volunteers were called for. Students, farmers, workers, government employees and soldiers were mobilized to meet the danger. Three hundred thousand men and women entered the battle. The flood fighters were organized like an army. Engineers were assigned to each division. The provincial governor, the party leaders, trade union officials and military officers were at their posts day and night. High winds drove great waves against the dikes, which gave way in places. Deeds of heroism were performed. Lives were lost. But the reinforced dikes held. After four long weeks the rain stopped, the sun came out, and the battle was won. Only the united, organized, ceaseless efforts of this flood-fighting volunteer army had prevented a major disaster.

Flood control projects, if successful, will reduce flood losses, provide hydro-electric stations, improve river navigation, furnish increased water for irrigation. Perhaps no single reform put into effect by the People's Government since Liberation has done so much to win and hold public interest and confidence as flood control. For the first time in written Chinese history, the people are becoming masters and not victims of their rivers.

We were so fortunate as to see the beginning of a flood control project in Central China, near Wuhan. Both the Yangtse and the Han Rivers flood in the summer. Flood water in the Yangtse rises 60 feet above the low water level. The Yangtse at Wuhan is nearly a mile wide, has a swift current, and in flood is 130 feet deep in mid-stream. Dealing with the Yangtse is no child's play.

Where the Han joins the Yangtse there is a large area of lowland which is regularly flooded. The 60,000 people who live in the area not only suffer from flood damage, but sicken and die from the presence of a parasite that survives in periodically flooded land. After years of discussion and planning, it was decided to build a circular dam around this area between December 1957 and March 1958. We were in Wuhan in mid-December.

106

One day as we crossed the new and splendid Yangtse bridge which links the cities of Hanyang, Hankow and Wuchang, we met a column of students, four abreast, swinging camping equipment and extra clothing from bamboo poles across their shoulders. The column of several hundred young people stretched out for blocks. It was a Saturday morning. "Is this a weekend camping party?" we asked. "No, indeed," was the answer. "These young people are going up to work on the new circular flood control dam, several miles from here. They have quite a walk ahead of them. This is a replacement shift. Every two weeks new volunteers go to this project. On their way they will pass others who have finished their two week shift and are returning."

We decided then and there to go to the spot if we had to walk ourselves. Bright and early next morning we were provided with rubber boots and a British jeep and were out at the dam site in company with one of the responsible engineers. It had been raining for days. The place was muddy, but the sun was bright. It was a sparkling day.

With the aid of a contour map we were given a picture of the whole project. Dikes already existed along the Yangtse and the Han Rivers. The circular dam, connecting the existing dikes, would close the gap and exclude flood water from a large portion of land. Construction surveys had been made, levels established, the lines of the dam staked out with long bamboo poles, cuts and fills were determined and grade stakes set.

Students, office workers, government employees, soldiers, peasants,—all volunteers, were doing the work. We know that it is difficult for Westerners to understand mass volunteer labor, because they have been taught to call it slave labor and to believe that all volunteer mass labor belongs in that category. In emergencies due to war or fire or flood, Westerners may volunteer and take a hand for brief periods. Once the emergency is over, however, they sink back into individualistic indifference to broad social needs. We can think of no Western country where a call for voluntary labor on a long-range peacetime government project would win the cooperation of more than a few hundred socially-minded people who could see the project as a whole, its relation to social well-being, and who would gladly cooperate,—giving time, energy, and sometimes sacrificing money and family to help in the larger scheme. The Chinese respond readily to calls for group work projects and are busy with such jobs all over China.

On the day of our visit to the Wuhan site, 60,000 workers were building the circular dam. The rain-soaked soil was too soft for heavy machinery. All work was being done with spades, mattocks, and baskets hung on the ends of bamboo carrying-poles. Each reed basket held three to four shovelsful of heavy clay soil. As the baskets were filled, the carriers hooked them onto their poles, raised them to shoulder height, and with each arm balancing a basket, proceeded at a fast walk or trot to the dumping points, chanting the while a sequence of short musical grunts.

The dumped earth was rammed into place by heavy wooden blocks attached to bamboo poles. Eight to twelve men or boys handled each tamper. A crew leader called out a slogan, "Here's to it, boys! Let 'er go!" Then he and the crew raised the tamper shoulder-high, and with a shout released it.

On our visiting day, there were 12,000 students, government employees and soldiers, and 48,000 peasants on the job. The peasants received one Chinese dollar, plus food, for an eight hour day. The soldiers got their rations. The students and government worker volunteers paid for their board and

108

got no wages. Most of the workers were men. Many were young boys and girls. Each group of volunteer workers came for a shift of 14 days. The peasants could stay on for the duration of the job.

Before a group of volunteers went to the dam site, their elected representative visited the project, reported the number of workers for whom he spoke, and arranged for quarters in the temporary barracks. Volunteers were divided into work teams of 700. Sub-teams containing 100 were divided into squads of 10 each. The squads selected their leaders. Qualified organizers headed the teams and sub-teams.

We stood on top of the 65 foot high river dike and followed the row of center poles with our eyes. As far as we could see there were work teams, sub-teams and squads. "How many people are at work right down below us?" we asked our engineer guide, indicating a wide circle. "There are ten work areas at the moment on the whole job," he answered. "Between six and seven thousand people are at work in this area. Next week we expect to have 100,000 volunteers working in 15 to 18 areas. The work must progress quickly. By March the farmers will begin their planting. We must put the rip-rap and other finishing touches on the project before that time."

We watched the ant-like scurrying groups of blue-clad figures who covered the ground below us and filled the air with their musical chants. It was a wide canvas and a fit scene for a Breughel to paint.

We went down over the curve of the river dike to the meadow level where only the first few feet had been filled in by previous squads. We walked over to a group of girls who were digging and hacking away at a mound of earth just outside the limits of the dam. When we asked for the privilege of handling some of the earth ourselves the smiling

109

girls handed over shovels and we dug in the good brown earth for a while and filled baskets.

Dodging trotting earth-carriers on the way, we walked over to some lads who were pounding down the dumped earth with tampers. The boy's leader smiled and waved, while the others cheered the arrival of foreign observers. With mighty slams they worked the tamper.

Toward the end of our visit the whistle blew for lunch and all over the vast field of operations the teams stopped work and gathered at various feeding depots where soup, rice and vegetables were ladled out in dishes, pans, cups and bowls. Those nearest us clustered round to look over the new arrivals. The crowd was friendly and curious. We tried English, Russian, German and French on them. Most of the replies were in Chinese, but elaborated with smiles and handshakes. As we turned to go, a lad called out in good English, "Tell your people at home that we want peace and friendship." We called back and waved at him. With the others, he stood waving until we disappeared over the top of the dike.

It was easy to understand the enthusiasm and ardor of the volunteers in this collective enterprise. The plan was before them in their mind's eye. They saw the dam rising inch by inch. Each basketful made a minute difference in the level. Each day's work began at the level reached the previous day. Each day's work showed as the earth-mass grew. All were helping together at a project they could understand and for an object in which they believed. At night they would sink into sleep, tired, but happy at the work accomplished and eager to do their bit again the next day.

We would have liked to stay longer (for hours or days or weeks) helping in this joint effort to build a dam and stem the floods. Not only would we have enjoyed the work and the physical exercise (as those others were enjoying it that day) but the exhilaration of being a small part of such a vast cooperative effort was tingling and heart-warming. We left the place with real regret. It was a finer sight than the Taj Mahal or Niagara Falls. It was a living contribution of willing hands to a socially necessary task. Tens of thousands of people, organized and well-led, working on a planned project of which they understood the importance, equipped with only shovels and baskets, accomplished wonders in 14 consecutive work days. Since Liberation such projects have been organized, started and finished off, one after another, all over People's China. Many others are still in the making.

We were looking over the new Wuhan Bridge across the Yangtse in Hopei Province. The bridge is particularly useful as it connects the several parts of the three river-divided cities of Wuhan—Hanyang, Hankow and Wuchang. It is an imposing structure built on nine piers anchored by piles into the rock of the river bed, and is nearly a mile long. It carries two railway tracks, six auto traffic lanes and two sidewalks on its two levels. Hills on each bank were partially cut away for the bridge approaches. All of the work on the approaches and much of the bridge work had been done by volunteers. "What sorts of people were these volunteers?" we asked. A poet, who was also an official, answered "All sorts"; then mentioned casually that he himself had put in a year on the bridge job.

When floods occurred in pre-Liberation days the laissez-faire technique was to let the flood victims follow their own roads to survival, walking the highways until they found shelter, and begging until they were given food. Big floods drove out refugees by the hundreds of thousands. The People's Government follows a very different pattern, inspiring and leading joint efforts of volunteers to work at the projects before emergencies arise, and when there are emergencies, organizing the victims and providing for their needs as they would for equal numbers of soldiers.

In December, 1957, Vice-chairman Chu Teh addressed the National Water and Soil Conservation Conference in Peking. He pointed out that water and soil conservation was a colossal national task. "The loss of water and soil on 190,000 square kilometres of land," said he, "has been controlled since Liberation. This achievement has increased the people's confidence and provided a fund of experience for future work in this field."

"According to surveys," said Chu Teh, "1.5 million square kilometres of mountainous and hilly land (nearly one-sixth of China's territory) were subjected to soil erosion. Year by year this diminished the fertility of the soil and decreased the capacity to absorb water, reduced crop yields and caused droughts and floods. Big dams and other water conservation can only become really effective after water and soil conservation work is done," he declared.

Flood control by means of dikes and dams is at best patchwork, helping only to handle flood water after it has left the hills. Dams, catch basins, emergency spillways, canals and locks have their uses for power generation, transportation and irrigation. But deforested hills will produce flash floods that do vast damage. There is one way and only one way to hold water in the hills and release it gradually. That is to establish and maintain a green carpet of grasses, shrubs and trees over every available acre of the water-shed. Heavy grass sods and a thick carpet of litter and humus on the forest floor are the best reservoir with which to hold the melting snow and falling rain.

The People's Government tackled floods with dikes and dams. At the same time it organized a program designed to cover China with grasses, shrubs and trees. "Greenize China;

112

make the brown hills green" was the slogan. The drive is far advanced. Species have been selected, seeds collected, nurseries established. Greenizing China was part of the First Five Year Plan.

Each province, city, village and cooperative has its quota and its plan for fulfilling the quota ahead of schedule. One cooperative we saw near Hankow had a greenizing program which called for the planting of both fruit and forest trees. In 1956 the cooperative planted 600 fruit trees; in 1957, double that number. Their program for 1958 called for 6000 fruit trees. At the same time the cooperative forestry program was going equally well on a considerable area of bare mountain land, hardly useful even for grazing. "Our planting schedule for forest trees is well advanced," said the chairman of the collective. "Unless we have unforeseen set-backs, we will complete our five year program in three years. The people are interested. The work will surely be done ahead of schedule."

We drove through some hills along the middle reaches of the Yangtse River. Our guide was a veteran forester who had been trained in the Yale School of Forestry, in New Haven, Connecticut.

"You see those hills," he pointed on both sides of the road. "Three years ago there was not a shrub or a tree on them. Look at them now. The two-needle pine which was planted two years back is beginning to take hold. It has missed here and there; these places will be replanted, but the overall results are better than average."

As we drove along, we saw hill after hill carrying a low green cover. Two-needle pines were everywhere, building their root systems. After another year or two the young trees would begin to shoot up.

We had reached a point near an engineering college. It

was late afternoon. Long sun shadows lay across the fields. We heard singing, and looking up we saw a line of young people streaming along a path that led down from the mountainside. They carried spades and mattocks. In answer to our inquiry as to what the young people were doing, our friend pointed up the mountain. There in long symmetrical rows were small heaps of newly turned red-brown earth,—hundreds of spots.

"These students have assumed responsibility for the preparation of a block of tree planting," he said. "They dig the holes carefully, putting top soil on one side and sub soil on the other. When the small trees come from the nursery, they will put the top soil at the bottom of the holes, around the tree roots. The sub soil will fill in on top. This method takes a little time, but it pays in the long run."

We asked whether the trees could be planted without water. "Yes," he answered, "if the planting is done just before the rainy season."

We had seen a number of goats in the neighborhood. Would they bother the new plantings, we wondered. "That is a trouble for us," the forester acknowledged. "When these trees are young, grazing animals easily uproot and destroy them. We are trying to keep the animals out of the district."

Our guide waxed eloquent. "Here we are with a program to greenize the bare hills of China within ten years, and we will do it. The Chinese are the most reasonable people on earth. If you can convince them that something like reforestation or dam building should be done and can be done, they begin to do it, and it is almost impossible to stop them. They take it up with enthusiasm, work at it collectively, and keep at it until it is finished, no matter how long it takes.

"In fact," he said with a grimace, "sometimes two programs carried out with full force collide. While we are plant-

114

ing trees, another government department is advocating an increase in meat animals and dairy products, and other enthusiasts are pushing colleges and all manner of institutions and factories out of the cities and into the country. The grazing animals, the school buildings and the factories all take land which has been planted with our seedlings."

"Here is a major problem," he concluded. "We need forests. We also need more food for an increasing population. We need more schools and factories. However, China is big enough to resolve this contradiction. Whatever our decision, we must have a green China, and the people will help us make it so."

People's China has a program for controlling and using water. It has a second program,—greenizing the land. A third program is being conducted under the slogan: "Into the mountains."

China is rich in people but poor in cultivable land. Ages ago the valleys and fertile slopes were occupied. There remained about two-thirds of the land surface of China, covered by steep and high mountains. Three-fifths of China is at least 6,000 feet above sea level. Life seemed easier in the lowlands, so people had turned their backs on the mountains and settled in the valleys.

Yet the mountains presented endless challenges and opportunities. They were rich in minerals, some underground, some on the surface. Almost everywhere in the mountains there was water power with which grain could be ground, cotton could be ginned, electricity generated and distributed. Some handicraft cooperatives were already established; others could be set up to use local raw materials. Herbs could be gathered. Forest crops of nuts and fruit could be harvested. The mountains were filled with undreamed possibilities for utilizing nature. Therefore, proclaimed the planners of the new society: back to the mountains!

A campaign was already under way while we were there to send capable young people from their city jobs into the countryside, where they could take advantage of the tempering effect of bread labor and could offer their skills and their book-learning to the villagers. Citybred intellectuals were volunteering by the tens of thousands to go out to the villages. Work on bridges and dams presented a challenge which young men and women from the city were accepting. This back-to-the-mountains concept involved an even more radical change in their way of life. We met personally many who were volunteering to spend years and perhaps the rest of their lives in the mountains.

Mountain life offered the Chinese people a widened and a tougher challenge, coupled with more than a touch of romance and adventure. City people had often read of frontier life in the roadless and trackless mountains. They had read of Europeans crossing the sea and treking to the Far West and to the Rocky Mountains in North America. Now they had an opportunity to explore, to discover, to build roads and houses, to develop areas which in many cases were without human inhabitants. China has its own wild west and its own mountains, its own opportunities for adventure, for opening up new sources of natural wealth, for greatly enriching the motherland. If a year or two in the villages was counted on to remake the city dwellers and leaven village life, an equal time spent in the mountains might do that and even more.

This concept of a whole people awakening to the benefits to be derived from linking mental work and physical work was one of the most spectacular developments we saw in China and one of the closest to our own hearts and way of life. Many years before, we had turned our backs on city life, had gone up into the Green Mountains, set up a subsistence homestead and established a frugal economy which enabled us to work outdoors at hard physical labor, to join our neighbors in cooperative projects, and to read, write and carry on our educational work. We thought it the only decent way to live,—a purposeful combination of work and leisure, of solitude and of sociability, a sharing and working together.*

In China we found a whole nation living simply and carefully, planning their periods of country and city living as we had done, recognizing the importance of physical and mental labor and of community projects, and striving to find a balance among all three. No wonder we felt at home as we never had in extravagant, gadget-mad, pleasure-mad, modern America.

As the First Five Year Plan moved toward a successful conclusion, millions of Chinese were adapting themselves to a communal way of life and thousands were leaving the cities (and all that that way of living implied) and were treking bravely and joyously toward the mountains. Like the valleys and the lowlands, the mountains were also part of China's good earth.

* The story of those years is told in our book *Living the Good Life*, Social Science Institute, Harborside, Maine, 1954.

117

3. ONE BIG FAMILY

Traditionally the Chinese people divided their loyalties between land and family. They drew their sustenance from the land; they organized their lives around the family. After Liberation, land reform and family reform proceeded side by side. Land reform aimed to provide a rational foundation for Chinese agriculture. Family reform aimed to emancipate the pre-Liberation family from the feudal remnants which still played so large a part in its organization and activities.

Another element entered the picture. Modern Chinese society, disrupted and divided for generations, needed a sense of unity and solidarity. The word "family" in China stood for both concepts. The Preamble to the Chinese Constitution of 1954 contains the sentence: "All nationalities of our country are united in one great family of free and equal nations." Leaders of the Liberation forces wanted to take the further step of making China one big family of free and equal citizens.

Long before Liberation, Chinese communists and their co-workers on the left had been telling the Chinese people that collective enterprise, aimed to promote the general welfare, would bring to each individual more of the good things of life because the community would have more good things to distribute. Such a doctrine was easy to promulgate among the Chinese because the enlarged Chinese family, amounting in some cases almost to a clan, was in many ways a common enterprise conducted for the advantage of all family members.

118

Since Liberation, the principle of collective enterprise for collective advantage has been extended until it applies to all members of the community, including those who prefer not to take an active part in building socialism. Each advance in the economic and social standards of living, such as better food, clothing, homes, schools and highways, sooner or later must benefit every individual and every section of a progressive, rational community. This principle of collective enterprise for collective advantage is the north star of those who are building the New China.

Collective effort for collective advantage found a logical application in land reform. Having established the principle that China's millions are part and parcel of one big family in which a benefit to all is a benefit to each and an injury to all is an injury to each, the makers of China's policy turned to specific measures, or, as they are called in China, "reforms." Among these reforms, top priority has been given to land reform.

Before Liberation probably nine-tenths of China's population lived by part-time or full-time work on the land,—by hunting or fishing, by forestry, animal husbandry, cultivation. Through the centuries three things happened to the land. It had been divided and sub-divided into tiny fields and strips, many of which were so small that they could be worked only by hand tools. Individual ownership not only made many land-workers landless and gave landlords a source of unearned income, but it reduced (close to the zero point) the probability of collective large-scale planning and management. Such fragmentation of the land resulted in deforestation, erosion, floods, droughts, and to the absence of any general program for land reclamation and soil rebuilding. Land reform was designed by the planners of People's China to deal with all of these problems.

Land reform began before 1949 in the areas that had been liberated from Kuomintang control. It was in full swing from 1949 to 1952. It included three stages. The first might be called distribution: the allotment of land to those who were prepared to use it. This allotment of land included former land owners, who were given their pro-rata share of the land available for distribution, provided they agreed to work it. They were not permitted to lease it or to employ labor on it.

The second stage in land reform was collectivization. Land sub-division in China had reached a point at which it was no longer practicable or economical to operate many of the smaller fields even on a basis of hand labor. Therefore a drive was started to unify the land through the organization of agricultural cooperatives.

Land unification in cooperatives made possible the third step in land reform,—a broad program for the use of the land through irrigation, drainage, the digging of ponds and catch-basins for water storage; the use of the simpler agricultural machines; reforestation on the mountain land owned by the cooperatives, and the planting of successions of diversified crops. Land reform in China is now in this third stage.

We visited Huang Tu Kang village, a vegetable producing cooperative near Peking. The cooperative was organized in 1952 as a mutual aid group of eight families. By 1956 it included the entire township of 2,003 families, or 3,300 labor units out of a total population of 8,000 persons. It had developed irrigation, drained swamp land, diversified its crops and was paying its workers cash incomes equal to the wages of industrial workers in the neighborhood. Beside this cash, each cooperating family had its house, its own plot for garden and animals, and the possibility of buying food from the cooperative at lower-than-market prices.

120

At the time of our visit, in mid-December, this cooperative had 3,000 hot-bed sash built into temporary, heated greenhouses, in which tomatoes, cucumbers, chives, and many flowering plants, including poinsettias and begonias, were growing. The cooperative had 130 horse-drawn carts in which these products were taken to the Peking market. On the return trip, city wastes, including manure and garbage, were brought back, sorted and piled into large, moistened, ventilated compost heaps. After about two months these piles, properly matured, were distributed over the fields to fertilize the spring crops.

In this district, where irrigation is necessary during the growing season, the peasants had watered the fields with hand pumps. With such pumps two men could irrigate a sixth of an acre per day. In 1956 the cooperative put its investment fund (12 percent of annual gross income) into electric pumps, of which they had been able to buy and install more than 20. Two men with an electric pump irrigated 3 acres per day.

At the head of the welcoming committee that met us and ushered us into a room of one of the village schools, was Yin Wei-chen, the chairman of the cooperative. He had gone to work for the landlord when he was a boy of 14. After Liberation, along with all the landless peasants, he got his share of land in the land reform. When the cooperative was set up in his village, Yin Wei-chen was one of the first to join.

We asked him how he was elected chairman. He told us that each production team selected two or three representatives. These in turn selected a management committee of fifteen. (In 1957 four were women.) The committee met two or three times a month, and from its ranks, once a year, elected a chairman.

Yin told us that the cooperative had brought large increases in production to the area. The increased income had provided everyone with plenty to eat, enough to wear, housing, fuel, funeral expenses, sickness insurance, and two month's rest for women at the time of childbirth.

This cooperative had experienced the worst drought in ten years during the 1957 spring and summer. "Before Liberation we had a bad drought," said the manager, "Two hundred families had to leave this village and go along the roads, begging for food. This summer not a family left the village. Despite the drought, we were able to meet all needs."

"What was the most decisive step in the success of this farm?" we asked. Without a moment's hesitation Yin replied, "Unifying the small fields and establishing a central management. Technical improvements came rapidly when these two steps had been taken."

In order to keep busy the year-round, this cooperative had set up a noodle factory where, from their own soy and broad beans, they made and processed noodles which were sold for export as well as in China. Within five years the peasants in this village had stepped from insecurity, poverty and backwardness to relative stability and well-being, based on planned, organized joint action.

One cooperative whose land bordered a lake decided to make fish production one of its secondary crops. In December-February, 1957-58, their off-season, the cooperating workers built a dike out into the lake, carrying the stone and earth-fill in baskets. By building from both sides, they expected to have the project completed ahead of schedule. The new fish pond, stocked with the best varieties of fish, would cover several acres and provide an important supplementary source of food and of cash income.

We visited a cooperative near Wuhan. It was in the hills and we had to walk in from the main road. They had started as a mutual aid group of six families in 1951. At that time they could get 300 gin of rice from one mou of land. By 1953 they got 730 gin per mou. "This had much influence on the people around here," said Lo Hwa chi, the head of the first mutual aid group. Four more mutual aid groups joined in 1953. They became a cooperative of 21 families. In 1955 they were 181 families, with 350 manpower and 777 people. The last remaining rich peasants and landlords in the neighborhood joined up. In 1957 the cooperative was getting 889 gin of rice per mou as the norm, with 1,240 gin as top production. The cooperative had 45 sows; each family getting 5 piglets per year. The total area of the cooperative was divided into 890 mou of rice land, 370 mou of vegetables and 1,800 mou of mountain land on which they were growing peach, pear, apple and nut trees. In 1958 they planned putting in 6,800 new fruit trees.

Pre-Liberation agriculture has been transformed by land reform. The unified cultivated areas have increased greatly in size. Collectivization has opened the way for soil conservation, for planning, for crop specialization and variety, for division of labor and the many other advantages that grow out of team work and collective action for collective purposes.

Side by side with land reform went the reform of family life. Before Liberation, no matter what emperor ruled or which dynasty was in power, the male was superior, the female inferior. Women could not choose their mates nor could they aspire to a general education. The man was the head of the household; women were servants and chattels in their own homes, and often beasts of burden and maids-of-all-work from morning to night. Old age did not lighten their labors. Millions of Chinese women were circumscribed from birth. Their lives, like their feet, were bound. Their role in the family was inferior to the point of subjection.

Economically, the status of women in Old China could

hardly have been worse. They were non-earning inferiors. Any money they might handle belonged to their husbands, even though they might have brought it into the family as dowry or inheritance. They worked for their keep and in many cases received harsh words and hard knocks as their only reward. ("Old Stick" was a common term used for boss and husband alike.) There is a song of New China which reminds women of the time not long ago when they were "at the bottom of the heap." It goes like this: "The old society was like a dry well, black, bitter and ten thousand feet deep. At the bottom were all we oppressed people, and the women were at the bottom of the heap."

Liberation revolutionized the status of Chinese women. They took part, along with the men, in the discussion of the draft Constitution for the People's Republic of China. When it was adopted in 1954 it contained an article declaring that "women in the People's Republic of China enjoy equal rights with men in all spheres of political, economic, cultural, social and domestic life." Here was a prodigious change in status. When China "stood up," Chinese women were given a chance to "step out."

For the first time women could vote and hold office on an equal basis with men. In the First National People's Congress (the Chinese Parliament) there were 148 women deputies, or 12 percent of the total. A woman, Soong Ching Ling, was elected one of the Vice-Chairmen of the Standing Committee. In the township or district people's congresses, more than a million women are deputies. Many women are mayors and deputy mayors. Government Ministers and Vice-Ministers are women. Women are chairmen of cooperative farms, directors of factories, judges, scientists, engineers, artists, writers, teachers, administrators, doctors, bank officials. Women's aptitudes and inclinations enable them to

124

make real contributions to the social, political and economic life of People's China. In New China there is no exploitation of men by man, nor of women by men. All are equal in law and fact.

The new marriage law of 1950 aimed to destroy the feudal marriage system based on arbitrary compulsory arrangements and male superiority. It promulgated free choice of partners, monogamy, equal rights for both sexes, and protection of women and children. A nation-wide campaign was inaugurated to show how the old system of arranged marriage cost money and made trouble, while "young people making their own matches saves money and trouble." The object in a partner was no longer a rich spouse, but a progressive, intelligent, diligent and healthy worker.

The new marriage law gave women equal rights in the home and equal control over property. The new education provided girls and boys with the same opportunities to acquire skills and prepare for professions. Industrialization offered young women and young men equal pay for equal work. The agricultural cooperatives, paying wages in cash and kind according to work done, made it possible for village women as well as village men to earn an independent livelihood.

Women's organizations, established at every level from the village and the block to the city, the province and the nation, explain to women their newly-won rights and help to implement them. There is an organization in China, the All China Women's Democratic Federation, which is concerned not only with women's political and economic rights but with their cultural, social and domestic rights, and also with their duties (because duties are stressed equally with rights in this new society). This Women's Federation is a standing conference of representative women elected from

125

villages and city blocks up to national levels. The leading women organize in a village or city street, and elect one representative woman who attends city or district conferences. They in turn elect their delegates to county and province. The top leaders are the elected women cadres of the country.

The chief aim of the Federation is to educate and work with all women to help establish socialism in China. At the village level they give help and advice on children, house work, marriage problems, birth control. They instruct on current affairs, both local, national and international. They try to wipe out illiteracy, and have newspaper reading groups. They keep in contact with international organizations and send and receive delegates to and from foreign countries. They work in cooperation with public health departments, on sanitation and hygiene. They help in clean-up campaigns, such as those of the "four pests": flies, mosquitoes, rats, sparrows.

Chinese housewives have taken up with a will the movement which started among the women in North East China, to excel in the Five Essentials or Five Goods ("Wu-hao" they call them): (1) to manage the household with thrift and industry; (2) to foster unity and mutual help in the family and neighborhood; (3) to bring up the children well; (4) to keep the house and streets clean; (5) to study hard. Wu-hao helps housewives to take part in community work and political activities. It inculcates new objectives, a new social tone and new moralities. It is mutual help in a new field. Collective efforts for collective advantage in the family, and the new status of women as equals at every level of Chinese society, has provided women with new incentives calling upon them to assume new responsibilities and thus broadened their role in Chinese life.

Chinese planners and organizers have applied the principle of collective effort for collective advantage not only to the home and family but to many other aspects of social life. One of the most successful applications has dealt with the realm of national minorities, which, the Constitution of 1954 stipulates, shall have regional autonomy and the freedom to develop their own languages and customs.

People's China has sixty or more national minorities, with a total population of 35 million persons, or six percent of the Chinese population. Some minorities are thinly scattered through the Chinese population. Some are concentrated in relatively homogeneous geographical areas. The Chuang people, 6,500,000 in number, live mainly in the mountains of Kwangsi. They make up 37 percent of the population of that province and are the most numerous among the minorities.

Since 1952 the Chuangs have had their own self-governing area in Kwangsi, composed of 51,000 square miles (larger than the State of Ohio). By 1956, 98 out of each 100 Chuang peasant households had become members of agricultural producers' cooperatives. For the first time in their history the Chuangs have a written language. In 1957 the first Chuang newspaper made its bow to the public. These steps toward Chuang self-determination and self-development have led to the expansion of education, the reduction of illiteracy, to higher production levels and better living conditions for the Chuang people.

Before Liberation Chinese minorities were at odds among themselves. In many cases they were not only backward economically and socially but their stronger and more advanced neighbors exploited the weaker and more backward.

Immediately after Liberation the entire minorities problem was taken in hand. Chinese minorities had been badly treated in the past. If China was to become one large family, the minorities had to have special consideration. Beginning in 1951 and 1952 a Central Institute of National Minorities was established in Peking with seven branch institutes throughout the country.

We visited the Institute for Minorities in Wuhan which was founded in 1952 and enlarged in 1953. The directors had no established method of procedure to which they could turn. Survey teams were organized and sent into the areas occupied by the minorities. These teams reported on their findings and recruited students for the Institute. In 1957-58 the Wuhan Institute had 730 students of whom 130 were women. They came from 19 nationalities and ranged in age from 11 years to 61 years. Some were put in the Preparatory School, acquiring the rudiments of an education. A second group, consisting of public officials, heads of counties, judges of people's courts and other local officials, were enrolled in an upper school. A third training course prepared people who came from middle schools, who would go back among their fellow nationals, establish schools and take up teaching.

Work with the minorities was confronted by one serious obstacle. Many of them had no written language and therefore no literature. In such cases, the first task was to convert the spoken speech into written form and lay the foundations of a literature. In the earlier stages pupils were taught by Han people in Chinese, the Han language. As their written literature grew, minority languages were used in classes and taught by their own people. During the First Five Year Plan linguists prepared scripts for eighteen of the minority groups. (Some of the minorities, the Mongols, the Uighurs and the Huis, had written languages before Liberation.) By the end of the Second Five Year Plan, in 1962, written languages will be provided for all minority groups, including the largest minority group in the country, the 6,500,000 Chuangs.

The adoption of the new alphabet throughout all China (instead of the present complex system of ideographs) will reduce the more than 50,000 characters in the language to 30 Latin characters. This language reform is expected to simplify and speed up the learning of reading and writing all through the country, but will be specially helpful for the minorities.

Another basic problem for the new Minorities Institute was food. The Director told us that each minority wanted its own type of food, preferably prepared by its own members. This problem was met by having the members of each minority prepare and serve their own food.

There was a third problem. Some of the minorities had long-established antagonisms and feuds. This problem was the easiest to solve. After brief periods of hesitancy, members of the various minorities learned to know and like each other, to organize mutual aid groups, and entered enthusiastically into programs of cultural exchange. Each national heritage consists chiefly of living habits, art, song and dance. In all of these areas the eventual desire of the students to share their culture was stronger than antagonisms, where such existed.

"The Institute will develop in accordance with the needs of the minorities," said the Director to us. "So far we have five departments: languages, history, art and music, politics, and a normal school. In the beginning it was very hard to get students to consent to come here. Since 1954, however, we have received thousands of letters from young and old people who want to attend the school. Students here are very diligent. In other schools it might be necessary to urge students to study. Here we must restrain them lest they overwork. Heretofore they have had little chance to learn.

Now they eat up the chance. They are clever and work hard. They are able, after three months, to understand lectures in Chinese."

Through one and sometime two interpreters, we talked with students. They spoke in their own language; it was translated into Chinese, and then translated into English. We were fascinated by the appearance and vigor of the students, their friendliness to strangers, their will and ability to learn. One oldish man made a good effort to learn some English from us. In a matter of minutes a young girl from a remote province who was learning Chinese picked up a dozen English words and after a few initial mistakes, repeated them and used them correctly, with understandable pronunciation. "Goodby," she called after us, waving a newly-acquired American scarf, "Kom bag zoon." We have long forgotten the equivalent phrases she taught us, but we would warrant she will remember her first English lesson if we met again.

These students were not only eager and quick at learning, but they were filled with zeal to go back among their fellow nationals and help them to take their places in one big family building a peaceful, prosperous, socialist China.

Unity and solidarity in one big family are transforming many aspects of Chinese life lying outside the family and the nationalities. A Chinese friend holds a prominent position in a university. When we called on him he was assembling his teaching material for the following week. All of the teachers, instructors and assistants associated with the course on which he was working formed a de facto collective whose object was to prepare and present the best possible course from the standpoint of the subject matter and also from that of student needs. A general meeting of the collective had laid out the course for the entire term. Each week a meeting was held to develop a special plan for the following week. Within this general framework each teacher is expected to use initiative and ingenuity in presenting the subject matter to the students. The presentation of a university course thus becomes a collective enterprise.

Our professor friend remarked wryly to us, "In the good old days, a professor delivered his lecture and walked out of the school a free man until it was time for the next lecture. Now he must sit in a committee which prepares the outline and subject matter of which each lecture must be an integral part. During this process a full professor, like each instructor and assistant, must listen to and answer objections and must be prepared to self-criticise. After his lectures are delivered, he must meet with his colleagues, summarize the experiences of the past week, listen to comment and suggestion and be prepared to self-criticise once again. Then in the light of the new experience, collectively analyzed, he must take part in preparing the work plan for the ensuing week."

Many an intellectual, accustomed to going it alone, would find such a regime irksome, irritating and frustrating. But a member of any effective team, whether of athletes, actors, workers, technicians or scientists, soon learns that teamwork is the pre-requisite of successful performance. A star, no matter how brilliant, secures the best results by working in and with a team of which he is an integral part.

We discussed the theory of collective enterprise with one of China's top planners. "We Chinese are one big family,— 650 million of us," said he. "We have agreed to turn our backs on imperialism and face up to the problems of building socialism. This is the common purpose toward which all of us are striving. Our common purpose is composed of many specialized variants; it even includes contradictions. Not only do we have differentiated groups such as the peasantry, the

131

workers, technicians, engineers, scientists, writers, artists and government officials, but we also have our capitalists who continue to live on unearned income while most of us depend on our wages or salaries. Also we have our right-wingers. To be sure, they are only a small minority, but many of them are deeply-ingrained individualists and some of them would even like to restore capitalism. Also we have linguistic minorities with their local traditions, customs and varying cultural practices. All of these elements are a part of our one big Chinese family. All must be accommodated, fed, clothed, housed, educated and given a chance to lead rewarding lives.

"On its face, such a problem seems immense and unmanageable. But we do not attempt to deal with the problem as a whole," our friend continued. "We think of it as a whole, but we deal with it part by part. Organizationally, China is divided and sub-divided until you reach the basic or mass organizations. In the countryside there are the cooperatives, the women's organizations, the townships and the counties. In the cities there are the residential organizations on every street, the women's organizations, the trade union locals. Throughout the country the Party, the Youth League and the Pioneers are locally organized. Then there are special organizations: for peace, for Asian-African solidarity, for sport, for study. All of these are specialized sub-divisions of the one big family. All citizens of China, except the most stubbornly anti-social, belong in one or another of these organized groups, which in the aggregate are committed to our common cause of building socialism.

"Our one big family is a whole composed of many parts," our friend concluded. "We do not believe that one part is more important than another. As in any other organism or mechanism, each part has a task to perform. Total performance depends on the successful working of each part and of its coordination into the working aggregate. This relation of parts to whole and of whole to parts has been stated many times and in many ways down through the centuries. We are striving to give it concrete form in an age of scientific advance toward the mastery of nature, the organization and control of society and the development and creative fulfilment of humanity."

4. EDUCATION FOR ALL

One of the foundation stones of the Brave New World is full, free, educational opportunity for all, on equal terms. We have laid special emphasis on this point in our description of educational developments in the Soviet Union. Educational developments in People's China are even more noteworthy because so much has been accomplished in so short a time.

Wherever we went in China, people pointed with pride to their schools. They rejoiced in land reform and in the transformation of family life. They were proudest of the nurseries, nursery schools, kindergartens, primary schools, middle schools, colleges, institutes and universities that were beginning to function all over their vast land.

People's China tackled an immense problem when it set out to reform and expand its educational system. At the time of Liberation probably nine-tenths of the Chinese people could not read or write. In the countryside, especially, school facilities were meagre. Those which existed catered to the children of well-to-do and rich families. Children of the poor had little chance for any higher education.

We spoke with educators in China's largest city, Shanghai, whose population is approaching seven millions. The city was short of school rooms, of school equipment and of teachers. By doubling up existing school buildings, with a full complement of children each morning and another complement each afternoon, they had been able to get about 800,000 children into their 20,000 primary school class rooms. They estimated that another 75,000 or 80,000 children of school age were still unplaced in primary schools.

Shanghai's educational problem was matched in every Chinese city we visited. Educational facilities in the countryside were even less abundant than in the cities. However, China's planners were making major moves to expand and extend educational facilities so that in the shortest possible time the pre-Liberation nine-tenths illiteracy figure would be wiped out in China and the entire population would not only be literate but would continue studying to the limit of its ability.

"The principles of socialist teaching," said the educators with whom we spoke, "are to develop the talents of the children, to teach them to think and to show them the problems they will have to tackle to build a socialist economy. They are shown the past, the present and the future. They must pick their own way. They will be the workers and citizens of tomorrow.

"We place great emphasis on physical training and cooperation within the community," they said. "Before Liberation the health of students was poor. Now they are sturdy and brawny. Students go on holidays to help pick fruit, dig turnips, and do other such outdoor work. Last week 59 boys and girls from one of our schools went to a cooperative to help build a small road. The young people are brought into

134

the life of the community, not left to play on the streets and grow up unprepared for the responsibilities and duties of adult life."

One of our first excursions in People's China took us to a primary school in Peking. As there were over half a million primary schools by the end of 1957 it was easy to find one to visit. This first primary school that we saw was a six year school, with 766 students, divided into 18 classes. Attached to the primary school was a kindergarten with 163 pupils.

Our visit was made on the morning of a December day when Peking weather is not very different from that of New York City. Perhaps the outside temperature that morning was around 25° F. As we went from room to room we found windows and doors wide open. When the teacher spoke and when the children recited, their breath steamed into the cold classroom air. Everyone was dressed in the customary Chinese winter garb,—heavy underclothes, sweater, trousers and warm cotton-padded jackets. It was practically an out-door school.

The school buildings, all of one story, surrounded a quadrangle that might have been 200 feet square. In the quadrangle, two classes were busy with setting-up exercises and group games. Except in stormy weather the quadrangle served as one of the classrooms, under the direction of the physical culture professor and his assistant, both young men. Students came and went with every change of classes, so that children from two or three classes were constantly exercising in the open air. Head work, hand work in the simply equipped laboratories and shops, and foot work (outdoor exercise) were part of the daily routine. We watched the students playing their skipping and jumping rope games, their ball throwing and their calisthenics, which they did with skill and vigor,

135

and later saw the same students quietly intent on their lessons in the schoolrooms.

The kindergartners were a delight to see, bundled but active in their padded jackets. Their ruddy faces, big dark eyes and welcoming smiles captivated us as they clapped their hands, sang their songs, played their games, told their stories and recited their simple verses. We could have spent all morning happily in their kindergarten rooms.

The school director, a strapping, sweet-faced, middle-aged woman, had the respect of both students and teachers. She was a fine human being, an experienced educator and an able administrator. The teachers, about equally divided between women and men, were quiet and competent. They told us that with new text books and better equipment, study results were improving daily. Before Liberation 700 characters were learned by the end of the second year. Now, 1,500 were learned in the same time. The children were avid readers and their growing appetite for books and general education was a challenge to writers and to all engaged in child education, welfare or cultural work.

Chinese middle schools correspond with United States high schools. After six primary years, there are three lower and three upper middle school years. In Shanghai we visited an upper middle school built in 1954-55. It would compare favorably in architecture, space and equipment with many an American school built at the same time. We pointed out to each other the school benches and desks and even the identical electric school clocks which reminded us of those at home. There were 832 students (201 girls and 631 boys); 36 teachers and 31 staff members, including cooks and waiters. There was a school director, responsible for administration, and a dean, responsible for education. The school had 18 classrooms and 6 special rooms, including biology, chemistry and physics laboratories and a well-appointed dining room and kitchen.

For each of the 18 classes there was one teacher, responsible to the director. Each class was organized under a class committee of 3 to 5 members, elected by the students of the class. All of the students in the school were members of a student's union with a standing committee of 11 members, elected by a student congress of 75 to 80 members (with 3 or 4 elected from each class). "Class elections and school elections are held twice each year," the director said to us. "We practice democratic centralism, thus the students learn how to govern themselves. All of us are members of society; our school is a part of that society and should not be separated from it."

About half of the students were members of the Youth League. These were the more mature, responsible and socially conscious girls and boys. We met the girl secretary of the League in this school. She told us, "There is a Youth League branch in each middle school. It is an independent political organization, with national, provincial and municipal executive committees. Students who wish to join must be good in studies and in conduct. We volunteer to plant trees. We help build Pioneer Houses. We do farm work with the peasants in the summer, as well as camp, boat, swim and hike."

Students were responsible for keeping rooms in order and also for keeping their part of the hallways clean and neat. On the day we visited the school we were not expected, as there was a mix-up in dates. The schoolyard, the school building, the rooms and laboratories were immaculate.

We went into classes in Russian, physics and the Chinese language. The teachers continued with their lessons. Not

137

a student turned toward us unless we were introduced. Attention and interest were on their work.*

All teachers and staff are members of the Education Workers Union. Membership is voluntary, but benefits are so extensive that membership is nearly universal. Union members pay one percent of their salaries as dues. "We have rights and obligations," said one teacher to us, "but our rights are much larger than our obligations." Teachers need not worry about unemployment. They get free medical service and pensions. Their wages are increased every second year, sometimes as much as 12 percent. Rents are low,—3 to 5 percent of income. Movies cost around 20 Chinese cents per ticket. The teacher's salaries will provide food, clothing and housing, movies, theatre and opera, a bicycle and other amenities. In the summer of 1957 the director and dean told us they both took a trip to Shenyang. This trip would have cost non-union members 30 to 80 yuan, depending on accommodations. As union members they paid 20 to 30 yuan.

Parents of students in this middle school (and generally throughout the country) were organized. There was one parent representative from each class. They met two or three times each term, 90 percent of the parents so delegated attending. Special meetings might also be called at the request of the school director or of the student union.

Before Liberation there were only ten middle schools in the three cities of Hankow, Wuchang and Hanyang. In 1957 there were 56. We spent a morning in one of their upper middle schools which had 1,364 students, all girls. We asked what proportion of the girls went on to university or insti-

* After our visit to People's China, back in Moscow, we commented to a librarian friend on the keenness with which Chinese young people were studying. She nodded approvingly. "Yes," she said, "I think they work even better than our young people. We have a saying in Russia, 'to study like a Chinese.' "

tute. "This year," they told us, "80 percent of those graduating will go on." We asked about the study of English. They said that Russian was the only foreign language taught in this school. English, however, was planned when enough teachers of the subject became available.

We said on a previous page that Chinese middle schools correspond with United States high schools. There are differences. Here are some of the subjects covered by a 19 year old graduate from a senior middle school in Tientsin. The girl is a daughter of a friend of ours. She has just finished a six year course. She has had five years of chemistry, five years of physics, four years plane and solid geometry, two years of trigonometry and four years of algebra. This is not unusual, as our friend's son passed through the identical courses a few years before.

Since returning home, we have received a letter from a friend in Peking. Her daughter attends the Foreign Language Institute there. It aims to train for translating, for scientific work, teaching, for foreign embassies and for foreign office work. (The Foreign Ministry has a special institute for training diplomats, where foreign languages are also taught). The mother wrote us, "I have had X . . . , my daughter, write out a list of subjects required in her classes. She is in the fourth year.

"Required subjects: analytical reading, home reading, reading aloud, oral conversation, two-way translation.

"Elective subjects: lexicology, poetry (she is now on *Paradise Lost*) and a second foreign language, which in that school means Spanish, French, German or Russian. She already finished majoring for two years in Russian at the Shanghai Russian College, so has over-fulfilled her foreign language requirements. Now she is taking two French courses, first and second year, but without credit.

139

"Other subjects for the whole four year course: English literature, grammar (3 years), phonetics, linguistics, geography, history of England, history of international relations, Chinese (ancient and modern) and politics (4 years).

"Research subjects: English literature, composition and history of the English language. (She is now reading *Chaucer* in Middle English!)."

We visited the Institute of Foreign Languages in Shanghai where, up to 1956, only Russian was taught. Now English, German, French are being introduced. The school aims to train translators and interpreters. The students study chiefly foreign languages, but also have classes in the Chinese language and in political science. Phonetics is stressed in the first, second and third years, as well as grammar. Vocabulary is the main object of the fourth year, and translation in the third and fourth years.

The Russian department has 800 students, taught by 100 professors, lecturers and assistants, 36 of the teachers being Russians. The Western language department has 100 students, with half the number of teachers, 8 of whom are foreigners. Students at the Institute pay no college fees and the majority live at the Institute for the four year course. No other special institute for foreign language exists in Shanghai, but there are courses and departments in other institutions. "The period 1952-56 saw Russian as an almost required middle school language. That spilled many Russian speaking enthusiasts into our Institute," said the friend who was showing us around. "In 1956 came the demand for English, and now for German. For the moment there are not enough graduates to supply colleges and universities with language teachers. That is the present big job,—to train new teachers."

Higher education in People's China was reorganized in

1952. Specialties such as language, medicine, engineering and agriculture are taught in colleges or institutes, which also carry on research. Universities aim to train top-level scientists, researchers and teachers. The linguists are trained in the Foreign Language Institutions; the teachers and the literary side of the languages are taught in the universities.

Peking University trains specialists for research and teaching work in the fields of theoretical science and basic sciences, both natural and social. New buildings are going up all over the Peking campus. We were shown their library which, since Liberation, has doubled its stock of a million books to near two million. Laboratories have increased from 20 to 210. All tuition is free, as well as room and medical care. Sixty to seventy percent of the students get scholarships covering board.

Reorganized in 1952, Peking University has fourteen departments, including mathematics and mechanics, physics, chemistry, biology, geology, geography, history, the Chinese language and literature, the Russian language and literature, Western languages and their literature, philosophy, economics and law, library science, with a special training course in the Chinese language for foreign students. (379 foreign students were attending in 1957.) There are 1,209 members of the teaching staff and 8,424 students. Women students are 21 percent of the student body. Students of worker and peasant origin are 22 percent. Student enrollment is three and a half times the number at the time of Liberation. Teachers are six times as numerous.

Among the colleges we visited was the Shanghai College of Finance and Economy, with a faculty and staff of 700, including 147 professors and assistant professors, 120 lecturers and 132 assistants. The college has five departments—financing and banking, accounting, statistics, industry, trade and commerce.

There were 1,500 students in day classes and 1,700 in evening classes. Twenty percent of the students (and 15 percent of the faculty members) were women. Before Liberation, the students came from bourgeois, landlord and government official families. Now 20 percent are of worker and peasant origin, the percentage increasing each year as more and more children of workers and peasants graduate for the first time from the lower schools. Eighty percent of the students get scholarships covering tuition, board, lodging and medical services. Twenty percent pay very moderate fees for board.

We asked what chance graduates had to get jobs. "In 1957," was the reply, "we graduated 200 from the accounting department. There were 800 jobs waiting. The situation is about the same in other departments."

China's agricultural colleges graduated a third more students in the past eight years than in the 40 years preceding Liberation. 150,000 people were enrolled in higher and secondary agricultural institutes during the First Five Year Plan. Courses included agronomy, fruit and vegetable growing, animal husbandry and veterinary work, tea growing, sericulture, plant protection, soil and agricultural chemistry, farm mechanization, farm management, water and soil improvement. All provinces in China, except Tibet and Chinghai, have agricultural colleges, almost forty percent of the students being of worker-peasant origin. Graduates in agriculture do farm work in rural cooperatives and state farms for one or two years after graduating before taking up future positions.

We were impressed by the workmanlike way in which preparations were being made for a large increase in educational facilities all over China. Peking is a typical capital,

142

with extensive government offices and installations in the heart of the city. On the outskirts an entire area is being devoted to cultural institutions dealing with all phases of education and research. On our first morning in China, while being driven around to see the sights, we counted north-west of Peking, within ten miles of the city, over a dozen different colleges, amongst which were the Colleges of Engineering, Mining, Medicine, Oil Prospecting, Music, Forestry, Politics and Economics, beside a College for Teachers, another for Post and Telegraph Workers, and an Institute for National Minorities.

Wuhan, a city of two millions, located on the Yangtse River in Central China, is developing a culture center around beautiful East Lake, a large body of water on the outskirts of the city. We stayed for about a week in a guest house across the lake from the University. Rarely have we been in more exquisite surroundings. Willow trees lined the lake and leaned over for reflection. Small peninsulas reached out into the water, with tiny templed buildings for wayfarer's repose. Fishermen's sampans floated by full-sailed or were rowed by rythmically bending figures. High on the surrounding hills were pagodas at sky level. The students' voices reached us across the lake. Early every morning, at dawn, the sound of their rising bells and their music for setting-up exercises came muted over the waters. The university buildings were architecturally lovely. Heavy green-tiled roofs with carved ornamentation added to the general artistic impression. We shall never forget the beauty of East Lake.

In 1949 Wuhan University and several small colleges were located in this area. In 1957, beside a reorganized university, the East Lake area contained a City Medical College, a Provincial Medical College, Central China Engineering College,

143

Central China Agricultural College, Central China Teachers University, Central China Institute of Music, Central South Institute of Finance, Central South College of Politics and Law, Wuhan Normal College of Arts, College of Water Conservation, College of Water Communication Engineering, College of Surveying and Cartography, a branch of the Central Institute for National Minorities, Central China College of Fine Arts, Wuhan Athletic College, Wuhan Normal Institute of Athletics, Wuhan Normal College. When Wuhan's center of cultural institutions is completed it will be the most extensive development of its kind in Central China.

Before Liberation Wuhan University provided a liberal arts education for sons of the well-to-do. Since Liberation the University has eleven departments aiming to develop scientists and teachers. "How many workers and peasant students attend the University?" we asked. "Before Liberation all students were from the bourgeois and landlord class," we were answered. "Now 40 percent of the students are from worker-peasant backgrounds. They all get free lodging and tuition; 80 percent getting scholarships for their board."

Wuhan's cultural expansion covers the entire range of education. In 1949 there were 4,490 students in Wuhan colleges and the University. In 1957 the students numbered 28,762, or six times the 1949 figure. During the same period, Wuhan Middle School students have risen from 17,587 to 88,200 and primary school students from 62,042 to 268,876. Such figures could be duplicated in all of the chief cities of People's China.

Some idea of the over-all advances made in Chinese education during the First Five Year Plan (1953-57) may be gained from the following figures, which give the number of students:

	1952	1957	Increase
Primary (to 13 years)	51,000,000	67,000,000	31 percent
Middle schools (years 14 to 18)	2,000,000	5,950,000	187 "
Middle vocational schools	380,000	740,000	95 "
Higher education	190,000	440,000	126 "

During the five years of the First Five Year Plan, 270,000 students graduated from higher educational institutions and 840,000 graduated from secondary vocational schools.

When we were in China, only eight years had elapsed since Liberation, and an even shorter time since the major educational reforms. Before Liberation, higher educational institutions were open almost entirely to the children of privileged families. During the ensuing years, the number of worker and peasant children in the school system has been increasing. This change is most noticeable in the secondary technical and vocational schools. In the 1950-51 school year, 37 percent of the students were from workers and peasant families. In 1957 the percentage had risen to 63 percent. Similar increases are expected in college and university student bodies during the Second Five Year Plan when the many worker and peasant students who began primary schools immediately after Liberation reach the higher educational institutions.

Chinese education is not yet entirely free. Middle school students still pay nominal fees and some students in higher educational institutions pay modest amounts for board. Rooms in hotels or dormitories are quite generally provided. Full, free education is the objective, and in the course of the Second Five Year Plan (1958-62) it should come close to realization.

People's China is keenly aware of its educational needs. Everywhere energetic efforts are being made to meet them. We began this report with a comment on the importance which socialists attach to the education and upbringing of their children, and gave some illustrations, drawn from our experience with children in the Soviet Union. The Chinese people feel an equal pride and have equal hopes for their children. Until we visited China we felt that the children we had met in Soviet Russia, taken as a whole, were the healthiest and best-balanced, pleasantest children we had seen anywhere. We now feel that the Chinese young people are at least the equal of the Russians in robust, sturdy, well-developed bodies and balanced minds. Outside of these two countries we have never seen young people, from babies up, who radiate such hope, confidence, purpose, self-possession and cheer. Chinese and Russian youth are climbing fast and far.

5. INDUSTRIALIZATION

China's one big family depends for its livelihood chiefly upon the land. For some years this dependence upon agriculture will continue. In the meantime an immense effort is being made to develop industry,—especially those heavy industries which produce iron, steel, coal, oil, cement; which manufacture railway supplies and equipment and build ships; which make machine tools, machines, trucks and planes and paper, and a great variety of light industry products.

Chinese industrialization has passed through four stages. (1) During the half century preceding Liberation, industrialization was largely financed and directed by foreign investors, businessmen and engineers. Mechanization was confined to a few of the chief cities. It by-passed millions of handicraft workers and hardly penetrated agriculture. (2) In the years

146

from 1949 to 1952, Chinese economy, severely damaged by invasion and civil war, was restored and re-equipped with machines and materials from abroad and under the supervision of many foreign (and especially Soviet) experts. (3) From 1953 to 1955, foreign-made equipment continued to pour into China and large numbers of foreign technicians remained there, but Chinese industries were turning out increasing quantities of machines and consumer goods under Chinese and foreign direction. (4) After 1956 Chinese industry was firmly on its feet, producing most of the needed consumer goods, equipping entire new factories with Chinese-made machines, supplying much of its own raw material, and carrying on, chiefly under Chinese direction, with some suggestions and advice from foreign experts. Specialized capital goods were still being imported.

We visited an important iron and steel complex in Anshan, North East China, which had been chiefly responsible for providing the structural iron and steel for the Wuhan Bridge over the Yangtse, opened on October 1, 1957. Besides being an important producer of iron and steel in its own right, the Anshan complex was also the mother plant which would supply China's new iron and steel mills with the machinery and personnel needed during the earlier stages of their development.

Anshan's iron and steel plant was founded by the Japanese as part of their program for the industrialization of Manchuria and North Korea. It was established as a unified iron and steel complex with a number of autonomous, functional departments. Under Japanese management the engineering and technical staff as well as the administration was Japanese. Iron and steel making in all of its aspects was top secret. Chinese did the manual work; Japanese monopolized the know-how. When the Japanese surrendered in 1945 and the Kuo-

147

mintang took control, the Anshan plant was like a headless body. The know-how disappeared.

Japan's peak production year in Anshan was 1943:— 1,350,000 tons of pig iron and 840,000 tons of steel. During the next 22 months, under Kuomintang management, the plant turned out 120 tons of steel and no pig iron. The skeleton of the Anshan plant was liberated in 1948. From 1949 to 1952 the factory was renovated and rebuilt. In 1953 it began production under the First Five Year Plan. Production for 1956 was 2,800,000 tons of pig iron and 2,310,000 tons of steel. This was twice the pig iron and nearly three times the steel production achieved by the Japanese at their highest output levels. In 1957 nine large blast furnaces and one small furnace were turning out pig iron. Four Martin ovens were making steel.

After Liberation the Anshan plant had plenty of manpower but was woefully short of managerial and technical personnel. At this point the Soviet Union entered the picture with trained specialists, skilled workers, with machines and even materials which were in short supply. Other people's democracies lent a hand, but the bulk of the assistance came from the Soviet Union.

Beside direct technical aid from Soviet specialists who went to China and spent years helping to put this and other plants into efficient production, the Soviet Union invited Chinese students of science and engineering to attend Soviet educational institutions. They had Chinese personnel from Anshan and other plants working in Soviet plants to learn what they could of Soviet techniques through first-hand experience.

Production plans for the Anshan complex for the period 1953-60 called for an increased volume of production and increase in the variety of products. Total items to be produced in the complex by 1960 were listed as 48. By the end of 1956, 31 of these items were being made.

Production has increased markedly in the Anshan plant. Wages have gone up even faster. Average wages in 1949 were 17.6 yuan per month; in 1952, 52 yuan; in 1956, 80.6 yuan.

Equally important has been the advance in worker-welfare. The Anshan plant is unionized throughout. Almost all workers, except the very young ones, are members of one or another of the trade union branches organized in each department. The trade union is responsible for maintaining and increasing production, for safe-guarding health and safety, for social security. The plant has its own program for the well-being of its workers. It is engaged in a large-scale housing development. It has built nurseries, kindergartens, hospital facilities, clubs and reading rooms. Each department of the plant conducts its own school for training young workers. Most of the new workers come from the farms. To prepare them for their tasks, the plant maintains two full-time technical schools and two spare-time technical schools. It also operates an evening engineering college which offers a six year course. Ten thousand students attend this college.

"Our workers are anxious to learn," the trade union chairman told us. "About 70 percent of them are studying in one or another course to improve their qualifications. The social basis in China has been backward," he added. "We have much to learn and far to go. But we have decided to go forward toward socialism and to do it all together. The workers know from experience that for the factory, as for the individual, increased efficiency will result in higher living standards. They are planning, thinking and working for better production. Between 1952 and 1956 suggestions for improving processes and working conditions have numbered over 30,000."

149

We asked the chairman about the pattern of trade union organization. The basic unit of organization is the work team which varies in size with the nature of the job. In a blast furnace there are ten or eleven in a work team. The team selects a leader and the leader speaks for and is responsible for the team. Each of the 63 units composing the Anshan complex, each factory, mine, mill, has its own trade union organization and a congress which is composed of one representative for each 20 workers. These departmental congresses elect representatives to a congress of the entire complex. This central congress meets once in six months. The manager reports to the congress and the report is discussed and suggestions are made. A congress lasts two or three days.

"We still have problems and difficulties," the chairman continued. "It is no small task to handle a plant like this, with its 63 different departments, including separate factories, mines and the like. But we have confidence in ourselves and the future. In the end, we shall conquer."

Conditions in the Machine Building Plant No. 1 of Shenyang, North East China, were similar to those in the Anshan Iron and Steel Complex. With 5,500 personnel, 20 percent of whom were technicians, the plant was turning out 4,000 to 4,200 large and medium sized lathes per year. The plant had been built by the Japanese in 1938 to do repair work and to produce springs and tanks. When the Japanese were driven out, they burned the factory. Kuomintang officials sold off much of the remaining machinery. In the winter of 1949 the Liberation forces took over the wreckage. It required four years to restore the plant, which reached full production only in 1955. Wages and welfare have advanced with production. There are eight wage grades: 36 yuan per month minimum to 110 yuan maximum. In addition to wages the plant paid bonuses equal to 20 percent of the wage total. Welfare funds provided by the plant equal 25 percent of total wages. Seventy percent of the workers live in model flats owned by the factory. The plant provides extensive educational facilities. It also takes care of 300 engineering students who are doing their practice work in the factory. When we were there all workers were engaged in summarizing and evaluating the work of the past three years as a part of the rectification movement.

Anshan was the largest industrial complex that we visited in China. Under the industrialization program equally extensive plants are being built, not only in heavily populated areas like Anshan but in remote mountainous regions of China's wild west. In these frontier regions, heretofore populated chiefly by hunters, woodsmen, herdsmen and farmers, teams of Chinese geologists and prospectors have discovered rich deposits of minerals and metals. Abundant water power and much petroleum completes a resource base upon which industry can be built.

Lanchow, in the province of Kansu, has been invaded by an army of engineers, building workers and technicians. For 1,500 years Lanchow had been a city made up chiefly of mud huts. Before Liberation a mud road connected Lanchow and its 200,000 inhabitants with the outside world. There was no railroad and the city had few paved streets. By 1957 Lanchow's population had quadrupled—to 800,000. Five railway lines radiate out from the city. Its broad central tree-lined avenues, some of them 150 feet wide, are being paved with asphalt. Kindergartens, schools, workers clubs, theatres, housing projects, beautified public parks and squares are being established to provide for the well-being and cultural needs of the fast-increasing population. Instead of growing like a straggling weed, Lanchow is developing according to plan as a socialist city.

151

Lanchow had only one bridge across the Yellow River before Liberation. Now there are four new bridges across the main stream plus 28 reinforced concrete bridges over the mountain streams that flow into the Yellow River in the neighborhood of Lanchow.

Before Liberation there were 67 elementary schools and 13 middle schools in Lanchow. Today there are 169 elementary and 30 middle schools. Higher educational institutions have increased from one to six.

Lanchow will be a green city. Streets, squares and parks are filled with trees, shrubs, flowers. Treeless mountain slopes surrounding the city are being afforested. Each inhabitant of Lanchow, to qualify as a meritorious citizen, must plant at least thirty trees a year.

Oil from West China will be refined in Lanchow. A giant refinery is scheduled to process a million tons of oil per year by 1959 and three million tons by 1960.

Near the refinery a plant in process of construction will produce the machinery, including turbodrills, required by the oil industry. The plant, covering 90 acres, will be operated by workers who are being trained in the industrial plants of 20 Chinese cities. Many of the qualified workers who will man the Lanchow plants have visited similar plants in the Soviet Union. This machine building plant is scheduled to open in 1959.

Beside oil products and machine tools, Lanchow will produce cement, agricultural implements, synthetic rubber, porcelain, chemical fertilizer and a variety of consumer goods.

A new thermal power station with a capacity of 300,000 kilowatts is in operation. A dam and a hydroelectric generation plant with a capacity of a million kilowatts is being built in a Yellow River gorge near Lanchow. This Lanchow dam, which is one of the 46 staircase dams that will control Yellow

River floods, will furnish power, transportation and water for irrigation.

Lanchow is one of many sites upon which People's China is building its industries. Geological surveys have discovered abundant mineral resources in China's mountains. China's abundant population assures the needed manpower. China's educational system is expanding to provide the technical training necessary to prepare the present generation for the speedy, planned industrialization of this important segment of the Brave New World.

We also saw some Chinese factories, opened in 1956 and 1957, that were planned, designed and built under the direction of Chinese engineers and technicians and equipped largely or wholly with Chinese-made machine-tools and machines. For example, there was No. 3 Textile Mill in Peking, which was Chinese throughout. It was one of the finest mills we have had the good fortune to inspect. "Our mill is entirely Chinese," the director told us, "but we had the benefit of Soviet advice in designing. The spinning frames, all made in China, follow a Soviet model which we have modified to suit our own requirements. Today the mill is operating efficiently with none but Chinese personnel."

Two exhibitions, one in Shanghai, the other in Shenyang gave us a general view of the industrial products of People's China. The Shanghai exhibit, showing manufactures for export from the Shanghai area, included a great variety of consumer goods and an extensive array of machines. The exhibit in Shenyang represented industry in China's North East district. In addition to machine tools, industrial equipment, textiles, chemicals, optical goods and the like, the exhibitors had erected working and semi-functioning models of largely automatic coal mines, of cement plants, paper factories and railroad equipment. These exhibits proved once

153

more (if further proof was necessary) that People's China was advancing with giant strides toward a place among the leading industrial nations of the planet.*

With the successful completion of the First Five Year Plan and the emphasis on the "back to the mountains" drive, industrialization entered a new phase. Beginning in 1958 the central government industrialization program was supplemented by a movement to build productive units which were to be planned, financed and constructed by provincial or municipal authorities. Within months this program began to bear fruit. From all parts of the Republic reports were reaching Peking of feverish activity looking to the local development of local units of the economy.

Where raw materials were locally available, small blast furnaces, shale oil plants, cement mills, chemical plants, coal mines, fertilizer factories and hydro-electric stations were being projected and started. Large enterprises, sponsored by the central government, were helping in the establishment of local small plants in their special fields. The national government was doing its bit in the same direction by producing 132 standard designs for various small industries and making the designs available for the guidance of local authorities.

Programs of decentralization, advocated for years by the Yugoslavs and urged at the 20th Party Congress in 1956 by Soviet leaders, won ardent support in People's China in 1957, partly because they were in line with Chinese economic tradition, and partly because they synchronized with the "back to the mountains" movement and similar reforms. In line with these policies, local enterprises were being encouraged to take more initiative and had been assured a wider range of autonomy during the course of their development.

* The Chinese Economy by Solomon Adler contains a wealth of material dealing with the industrialization of People's China.

154

Should these moves for the quick development of local enterprise proceed with the enthusiasm and the public support that have marked their earlier stages, many elements heretofore inactive, or only partly involved in the industrialization campaign, will participate in its fulfillment. These efforts, supplementing the program already sponsored by the national government, should add materially to total output, and thus speed plan over-fulfillment.

One further consideration justifies this stepped-up attack on the problems of industrialization. Big central plants require the assemblage of large amounts of material and labor power. Their construction covers years. Small plants can utilize local raw materials and local man power and can be completed in a fraction of the time required to put large plants into production. The program thus broadens and intensifies the campaign for industrialization and shortens the time which must elapse before the new units are put into production.

China's rapid industrial expansion will require millions of additional skilled, experienced workers, technicians, engineers and specialists, many of whom will come from the 75 million students now registered in Chinese schools and colleges. Industrialization and the partial mechanization of agriculture will require a great number and variety of tools and machines, many of which are now pouring from Chinese industrial plants. Meantime People's China is importing specialized tools and machines. Up to 1957, for example, the Chinese had made no attempt to produce passenger planes or automobiles. In December, 1957, they began turning out passenger planes, and in 1958 they expect passenger automobiles to begin rolling from the assembly lines. They cannot industrialize an agrarian economy all at once. It is necessary to take one step at a time. For years to come People's China will import some personnel and immense quantities of specialized producer goods.

Industrialization has only just begun in People's China. Much transport and much of the lifting and carrying in China is still done by human and animal muscles. But railroads are being extended and equipped. New deposits of fuels and metals are being discovered and developed. New hydro-electric projects are under construction. New roads are being built and old ones are being regraded, widened and surfaced. Thousands of bridges, factories, office structures and public buildings are nearing competion. Dwelling units are being constructed by the million. A great westward movement is taking place. Regions hitherto inaccessible except to hunters, trappers and herdsmen are being penetrated by roads and railways. New centres of population are mushrooming. The continent-wide development which covered two centuries of North American history will be far advanced in China by 1969, two decades after Liberation.

6. SOCIAL OWNERSHIP AND COOPERATION

Westerners who visit the beehive of activity which is People's China, invariably ask the question "Who owns all of this? Is there any private property?"

There is no easy answer to this question. Before Liberation there was public property in China such as the post offices; social or group property belonging to organizations such as trade unions and cooperatives, and private property in the hands of individuals:—land, houses, stores, factories. Private property, both in land and business enterprise, predominated. Since Liberation, land and other natural re-

156

sources and public utilities have become public property. Cooperatives in agriculture, in handcrafts and in trade are a prominent feature of Chinese economy.

Under the Constitution of 1954 property relations are described thus; "The ownership of the means of production today mainly takes the following forms: state ownership, that is, ownership by the whole people; cooperative ownership, that is, collective ownership by the working masses; ownership by individual working people, and capitalist ownership." (Article 5)

"State-owned economy is socialist economy owned by the whole people; it is the leading force in the national economy and the material basis on which the state carries out socialist transformation. The state ensures priority for the development of state-owned economy. All mineral resources and waters, as well as forests, undeveloped land and other resources which the state owns by law are the property of the whole people." (Article 6)

"Cooperative economy is either socialist economy collectively owned by the working masses, or semi-socialist economy in part collectively owned by the working masses. Such partial collective ownership by the working masses is a transitional form by means of which individual peasants, individual handicraftmen and other individual working people organize themselves in their advance toward collective ownership by the working masses.

"The state protects the property of the cooperatives, encourages, guides and helps the development of cooperative economy. It regards the promotion of producer's cooperatives as the chief means for the transformation of individual farming and individual handicrafts." (Article 7)

"The state protects peasant ownership of land and other means of production according to law.

"The state guides and helps individual peasants to increase production and encourages them to organize producer's, supply and marketing and credit cooperatives voluntarily.

"The policy of the state towards rich-peasant economy is to restrict and gradually eliminate it.

"The state protects the ownership of the means of production by handicraftsmen and other non-agricultural individual working people according to law." (Article 8)

"The state guides and helps individual handicraftsmen and other non-agricultural individual working people to improve the management of their affairs and encourages them to organize producers', and supply and marketing cooperatives voluntarily." (Article 9)

"The state protects the right of citizens to ownership of lawful income, of savings, of houses and the means of life." (Article 11)

"The state protects the right of citizens to inherit property according to law." (Article 12)

"The state may, in the public interest, buy, requisition or nationalize land and the means of production both in cities and countryside according to provisions of law." (Article 13)

"The state forbids any person to use his private property to the detriment of the public interest." (Article 14)

"By economic planning, the state directs the growth and transformation of the national economy to bring about the constant increase of productive forces, in this way enriching the material and cultural life of the people and consolidating the independence and security of the country." (Article 15)

Most property law aims to stabilize property relations. Under these constitutional provisions the basic property law of China aims to transform private ownership first into cooperative and then into public forms of ownership. It is one part of the general Chinese program for building socialism, step by step.

Between 1952 and 1956 there were several important changes in the property relations of Chinese economy. The most far-reaching was the planning, construction and organization by the public authorities of several hundred economic projects, all of which were within the public sector of the economy. The successful completion of the First Five Year Plan at the end of 1957 tipped the economic balance decisively in favor of public economy.

Public property is all but universal in power development, in public utilities, in banking and insurance, in communication. It plays a large role in manufacturing and transportation. New capital investments made in the fulfilment of the Five Year Plans are coming almost entirely from municipal, regional, provincial or national government sources.

Almost equally decisive, in the trend toward socialism, was the movement of the Chinese peasantry into three-quarters of a million agricultural cooperatives. In the same period, handicraft workers, who still play a large role in Chinese economy (especially at the village level) banded themselves into producer cooperatives.

We visited a building in Shanghai where artists and artisans were living and working together in a cooperative venture to keep alive and extend the ancient village crafts. We went from room to room where exquisite work was being done in paper cut-outs, rice paste sculpture, tiny ivory carving, feather work, and highly skilled crocheting and embroidery. Most of the teachers were old men or women who would have withered away in villages with little recognition and small chance of patronage or pupils in this modern age. Here

159

they were being given honor and recognition, were supplied with housing and emoluments, with materials and pupils. They were overjoyed that their lore would not die out. Talented young craftsmen were learning their skills and China's ancient arts would not be lost.

Among the most interesting experiences in China were our visits to agricultural cooperatives which had made small beginnings in 1951 or 1952 and which had mushroomed during the ensuing years.

"Have you been able to get all of the families in your neighborhood to join your enterprise?" we asked the chairman of one agricultural cooperative. "No trouble at all," he replied. "Once we got organized there was no question about our success after the work teams learned their business and the government paid us cash for everything we brought to market. Our members were receiving incomes which put them in the class of rich peasants. Beside paying our members cash wages, we were providing them with social security at the same time that we improved our land and equipped it with more machines.

"With us, social security means the provisions of the 'five goods': good food, good clothing, good housing, good education and good health services. Before Liberation, most of our members were deficient in one or more of these respects. Since 1955 we have been able to guarantee them to any family which would join our cooperative, who shared in the common labor, kept their homes in repair and cultivated their garden plots. Compared with the years before 1950, only a few of our members even dreamed of such security. Today no farmer in his right mind could stay out of this or some other cooperative. The last 17 families in this neighborhood joined our collective this year. They were former landlords and were holding out bitterly. However, even they finally saw the advantages of joining our group. Now all are in."

Where we asked about the relative welfare of the land workers before and after land reform and collectivization, we met the same answer, "Most of us have never had it so good. In our village since land reform only the landlords, the money lenders and a few of the richer peasants who had hired labor have suffered losses."

With the exception of a small minority of rich farmers and landlords, collectivization had opened up new vistas of technical advance that were almost entirely closed to the middle and poorer land workers under the private enterprise system. Cooperation has presented technical problems, but with the coming of social group enterprises, the individual has enjoyed a large degree of protection and security, not a little of which have been the immediate result of group pressure and group action.

Perhaps the most unique aspect of this planned, guided, peaceful transition of a private enterprise economy into a socialist economy dealt with trade, commerce and the manufacture of consumer goods. Generations of Chinese private enterprisers had occupied this field, not merely in China, but in other Asian countries where "businessman" and "Chinese" were all but synonymous. With Liberation came the question: what to do with the businessmen? If they were eliminated from the economy, many capable managers and much invaluable know-how would be lost. The obvious solution to this problem was to persuade the businessmen to continue at their posts and coexist with public enterprise. After a carefully planned and organized campaign of persuasion, the Chinese private enterprisers accepted joint enterprise and threw in their lot with the builders of socialism.

Legal justification for this development is written into the 1954 Constitution: "The state protects the ownership by

161

capitalists of the means of production and other capital according to law.

"The policy of the state towards capitalist industry and commerce is to use, restrict and transform them. The state makes use of the positive qualities of capitalist industry and commerce which are beneficial to national welfare and the people's livelihood, restricts their negative qualities which are not beneficial to national welfare and the people's livelihood, encourages and guides their transformation into various forms of state-capitalist economy, gradually replacing capitalist ownership with ownership by the whole people; and this it does by means of control exercized by administrative organs of state, the leadership given by state-owned economy, and supervision by the workers.

"The state forbids any kind of illegal activity by capitalists which endangers the public interest, disturbs the social-economic order, or undermines the economic plan of the state." (Article 10)

Joint enterprise as a form of property and business relationship came into existence early in the development of the First Five Year Plan. Certain segments of Chinese economy were socialized without question. In other segments the urgency of public control was not so evident. In these fields, government went into business with "good" capitalists.

"Good" capitalists are those who agreed to co-exist and work in harmony with a planned society which is building socialism. This co-existence will continue for seven years (1956-63) under agreements which make private business a partner of government. Assets are valued as of 1956. Thereafter, no additional capital may be invested in the business by the former private owners. If agreement is reached, the former manager is continued at his old salary. Stockholders are paid 5 percent on the agreed value of the property. If additional capital is required, the government invests it. Raw materials and equipment are provided, and prices and taxes are fixed by the government. The products of a joint manufacturing concern are sold to government trading companies. With these restrictions on sources of material, on capital and on markets, the government, with its taxing power, is in a position of control. As a partner in joint enterprises the government has access to the books of each concern. Thus the chances of deception are reduced to a minimum.

We spoke with several "good" capitalists. One and all agreed that their responsibilities were decreased, while their market was enlarged by planned economic expansion. Their incomes, both wages of management and return on investments, were virtually guaranteed by government. The risk of failures due to business cycles was eliminated. Labor troubles were almost non-existent.

A capitalist who owned a plant in Shanghai had another plant in Hong Kong. He commuted back and forth between the two cities. He said that his chemical company in Shanghai was going better and causing him less headaches than the one in Hong Kong.

"Practically speaking," said one of our capitalist informants, "we are under government supervision. Prices, wages, profits and interest rates are all fixed for us. During the period of joint enterprise, we cannot get rich, but neither can we be put out of business so long as we attend to our affairs."

Another joint enterprise capitalist epitomized the change of viewpoint that was developing in China under the new Peking regime. "Before Liberation people were concerned with income. Now they are more concerned with work."

Private property still plays a role in Chinese economy. Many families own their homes. Multiple family apartment houses which are being generally constructed in industrial cities reduce the possibility of private ownership, but in smaller communities there are many single privately-owned family dwellings. On this property, in the house or in an outbuilding, members of the family frequently engage in handicraft work or conduct a store or shop. This they may do if they employ no outside labor. In the countryside, members of agricultural cooperatives may build and own houses on plots of land whose size varies with the size of the family unit. Farmers raise crops or animals on plots of land assigned to them as household plots, and dispose of the products as they see fit.

The results of this five year co-existence between expanding socialism and contracting capitalism are noteworthy. By the end of the First Five Year Plan, the socialist sector of the economy was predominant in both country and city. Wagery (the purchase and exploitation of labor power) had been practically eliminated and private enterprise was negligible.

By the end of 1956 state factories and mines accounted for 65.15 percent of the gross industrial product, cooperatives accounted for 2 percent, and joint enterprises for 32.5 percent. State farms accounted for 1 percent of the gross agricultural output, agricultural cooperatives for 94 percent and individual peasants for 5 percent. State stores were doing 38.5 percent of the trading; supply and marketing cooperatives 29.9 percent; joint enterprise stores, 28.6 percent, and private traders 3 percent of the business. Transportation, communication, banking, the issue of currency, the production and distribution of electric energy were entirely in public hands.

Such results, achieved after only four years of planned economy, were due chiefly to the maintenance of a balance between the amount paid in personal incomes and the amount of available consumer goods; between the increase in production and in personal income, and between the incomes of farm workers and industrial workers. At the same time, the national budget was kept in balance. Prices and the purchasing power of money remained virtually unchanged.

Public property predominates in present-day Chinese industry. Collective or group property predominates in the Chinese countryside. Within five years private enterprisers have adjusted themselves to a period of co-existence with a dominant public sector. Chinese planners describe the trend toward public property and collective property as "socialist."

Experience in other countries which have begun socialist construction would lead an observer to conclude that the advance toward collective action in Chinese agriculture, industry and trade has been more rapid than even the most hopeful and enthusiastic could have anticipated. These profound changes in property and class relations have been made not only in record time but with comparatively little friction, disturbances or disorder.

7. HOUSE CLEANING AND RECTIFICATION

People's China inherited a house which was littered historically with scattered remnants of feudalism, considerable fragments of imperialism and segments of capitalism. It was cluttered economically with primitive methods of agriculture, inadequate transport (largely on human backs), unplanned industry (partly controlled from within China, partly from abroad), imbalance between city and countryside, inefficiency, inflation, excessive and unequal taxation, abysmal poverty. Sociologically and physically, Old China was filled with outmoded traditions, obsolete institutions, hard class

165

divisions, discrimination against minorities, virtual vassalage for most women, bureaucracy, corruption and just plain dirt.

In such a society any serious attempt to clean house would have infringed on the prerogatives and upset the vested interests of the landlords, capitalists, money-lenders, war lords and officials who held a dominant position in pre-Liberation Chinese society.

After the Chinese people "stood up" in 1949, a new ethic was promulgated and a new program adopted. The new ethic was "something for something,"—to each according to his product. The new program called for a planned, industrialized, socialist society, run efficiently and honestly by and for the people.

The general welfare came first; private interests were made secondary. The clever man who could get himself into a position to live on the backs of his fellows was no longer looked upon as a success. On the contrary, he was classed as an anti-social element. After land reform, landlords who had controlled the economic, political and social life of the Chinese countryside were replaced by the Party, the Youth League, and by spokesmen for the People's Government and for women's organizations. The new marriage law and the 1954 constitution liberated women. Nationalization and joint enterprise destroyed the power of private business. The imperialists were almost entirely out of the picture. People's China was a largely independent, self-determining society, under a new leadership which was dedicated to building socialism.

Before socialism could be established, however, the outlooks and many of the practices of Old China had to be changed or abandoned. The San Fan or anti-corruption movement was launched by the People's Government. It was directed at the three evils: graft, waste and burocracy. Po-

166

litical and financial graft, or "squeeze," had been taken for granted in Old China. When the People's Government outlawed squeeze, no one paid much attention to the ruling. Such reforms had been tried previously without seriously disturbing the grafters. The Government took a second step. "Squeeze, like every other form of graft, is unsocial," its spokesmen argued, "therefore squeeze has no place in a socialist community." Upon this proposition Party members, the peasants, the workers and the intellectuals were generally agreed. The third step followed promptly. Anyone who had been grafting, who realized the anti-social nature of his actions, who admitted his faults and was prepared to reform, would be dealt with leniently. As for the others, their names were on file, with a record of their mis-doings. If they did not confess, they would be brought into open court, their misdeeds would be proved and they would be given the extreme penalties provided by law.

By the time the campaign against graft was launched, the People's Government was recognized as incorruptible and had won general respect and wide popular support. Most of the grafters promised to mend their ways. The few who persisted got long prison terms. Within a short time squeeze and other forms of graft had virtually disappeared from Chinese public life.

Another anti-social element in Old China had been burocracy mixed with nepotism. Those who were clever enough to get themselves easy, well-paying jobs in the public service worked in their relatives, without much regard for training or fitness. The result was a top-heavy, lax burocracy, often corrupt and gang-ridden. The People's Government cleaned out burocrats and put government service on an efficient basis as well as an honest one.

Wu Fan was a campaign against the five evils: **bribery of** officials; evasion of taxes; stealing government property; cheating by supplying adulterated or inferior products; ferreting out economic information for private speculation.

Another element entered into the picture,—the age-old difference between the slow-moving, ponderous land worker and the nimble-witted, fast-moving city slicker. Four out of five of the Chinese people were land workers. Through the ages this majority of peasants had been ruled by the landed and other vested interests working hand in hand with the small minority of intellectuals, thus dangerously dividing Chinese society into contending and conflicting classes. Liberation had been effected by a united effort of land workers, industrial workers and intellectuals. If this unity was to be preserved, the gap separating land workers and city dwellers must be narrowed or bridged. The first steps, toward classlessness, land reform and the socialization of the economy had been taken. The next step,—equal education opportunity for all, was under way. There was a final and very practical step. City people, especially the intellectuals, should be transferred to the countryside for a period of tempering through labor and the exchange of cultural experiences.

Movement into the villages was not decreed for all city dwellers, but for "cadres." A cadre in People's China is a person who serves in an official or semi-official position. A trade union official is a cadre; so is a worker in the office of a trade union. The distinguishing characteristic of a cadre seems to be a white collar worker who is also an activist. It was the white collar workers from the cities who needed experience in village life and who could make the most effective cultural exchanges with village dwellers.

Complicating factors were inherent in the situation. The villagers could use help, but they needed less, not more, mouths to feed. The city people were not accustomed or trained to work on the land or in villages. There would be much psychological adjustment in such an experiment.

The movement of city people into the villages was in full swing when we were there in 1957. First came the period of persuasion during which arguments were presented in favor of the reform. There were speeches by government leaders, articles in the press and plugs on radio programs. Then discussion and argumentation went on in the offices, factories and shops. Only after the campaign had achieved its objective and people were persuaded that it was a good thing were volunteers called for.

Necessarily the persuasion campaign was two-pronged. City dwelling cadres had to be persuaded that it was important and useful for them to go to the villages. It was equally necessary to persuade the villagers that there were advantages to be gained and that they should welcome their guests from the cities and act as generous hosts. Both of these results were achieved.

After the persuasion campaign, the move into the villages entered its second stage—volunteering. No general figures were available as to the numbers of volunteers, but we knew of instances where virtually entire office staffs offered to go. Westerners frequently raise their eyebrows when they hear the word "volunteer" applied to work in People's China. Their image of China is a newsreel compound of drabness, uniformity, coercion and mass slave labor. Having been on the spot and having seen volunteering in action we know that enthusiasm ran high for this further experiment in socialist planning.*

* One of the questions we asked while in China dealt with the volunteers at the time of the Korean War. Did they go of their own free will, or were they drafted? The answers we received were all the same: they went of their own free will. One of the men to whom we spoke had charge of a trade school in which there were about a thousand young Chinese. When the

169

After volunteering came selection. A choice had to be made. Who could best be spared from the organization? Who needed the experience most? Who could contribute most to the life of the village? These matters were discussed at length in general meetings in which all persons engaged in a particular enterprise or department participated. Some offices were closed for hours and even days while these matters were being discussed.

Finally there was the question of assignment. Volunteers did not move *en masse* into the countryside. Each volunteer went to a particular village and to a particular billet in that village.

One organization with which we were familiar had a staff of about a hundred in its main office. After repeated staff meetings, the decision was made to send one-fifth of the staff to the villages at every two year period, so that in the course of ten years all members of the staff would have had an opportunity to be tempered by hand labor and to offer their city-acquired social skills for the enrichment of rural life. Those who went were to continue for the first year in the village at their present salaries. During the second year they were to be paid the same income as other villagers with equal skills. By the time the second year came around they would appreciate the villager's needs and problems and would know how to live on their village wages.

Final assignments from this office were made toward the end of December, 1957. Amongst those who had volunteered

students heard that United States-led armies were marching to the Yalu and that volunteers would be accepted, 95 percent signed up to go. "Those who did not volunteer," our informant told us, "were either too young or too incapacitated physically to endure the rigors of a military campaign. Of these 900 or more volunteers, only four went to Korea; the remainder stayed in school. The response across the country had been so overwhelming that only about one in each two hundred volunteers could be accepted."

with alacrity was a close friend of ours. He burst in upon us early one morning, beaming, with the news that he was among those chosen and assigned to go to a village the following month. The names of the lucky ones were posted; wall newspapers were filled with letters commending the chosen staff members and wishing them well during their next two years of village life. They were showered with congratulations as though they had just won a prize or gained some important social distinction (which indeed they had).

Our visit to the Shanghai College of Finance and Economy coincided with their selection of 65 out of a total of 700 faculty and staff members to spend at least a year in villages. Many more than the 65 had volunteered to go, but the urgent task of taking care of a greatly enlarged student body had limited selections to 65.

We have mentioned the reform of grafters, of corrupt and inefficient burocrats and of confirmed city dwellers who theorized without practicing. Several other reform campaigns were in progress: a campaign against gangsterism and racketeering, a campaign against the business and practice of prostitution, and a campaign against gambling, opium smoking and night clubs. All of these practices had been encouraged and patronized by profit-seeking foreigners and by the former ruling class elements. People's China put all of them under the ban.

Other campaigns directed by the house-cleaners of Chinese public life dealt with sanitation, drainage, vermin, dirt, disorder. On our last visit to China, thirty years before Liberation, we had been dismayed at the litter, filth, vermin and lack of sanitation in the larger cities. Ten years after Liberation we were astonished to see the transformation that had taken place. In 1957, Chinese cities compared favorably in these matters with the most advanced cities of the West.

New Year's Day is a great holiday in China. During the preceding week we were living in Peking. Early one Sunday morning, clean-up teams moved through our part of the city. Thirty or forty people carrying banners and flags made up each squad. A squad went along our street, stopped at a corner, set up a loud speaker, played some music, sang songs, and called upon the neighborhood to clean up in preparation for the New Year. Five minutes later the clean-up squad moved to another street and repeated the program. As the clean-up team left the place we were watching, people came out from the houses and buildings and began to sweep the street and the sidewalks. Children participated, picking up what bits of papers, scraps of wood or other litter they could find. As a matter of fact there was surprisingly little. Any Western city would look unusually clean with only the litter which the sweepers of Peking came out to clean up on that Sunday morning.

The next day we encountered dozens of girl Pioneers equipped with megaphones who stationed themselves along the chief shopping streets in our section of Peking. They stood in groups of two or three at the corners, calling out clean-up slogans and advising the passing throngs to spit only in spitoons and not on the street or sidewalks. The Chinese are proverbially hearty spitters and the girls explained the dangers of indiscriminate spitting.

Thousands of Peking citizens, young and old, were engaged in this pre-New Year cleanup campaign. According to all accounts, the campaigns against flies, mosquitoes and rats seem to have been equally well organized. In February, 1957, when we were in Bombay, we heard that city's mayor give a report on his recent trip to visit the mayor of Tientsin. He started his talk by a telling remark. "You have all heard that there is not a fly to be seen in China. I want to say that this is not true. I saw one. And everybody was after it."

Campaigning against dirt, against water pollution and food adulteration were parts of a much larger campaign in favor of good health. Before Liberation China had a high infant mortality, was a prey to infectious diseases and was scourged by plagues such as cholera, small pox and typhus. One of the earliest and most insistent reforms was directed against disease and toward health. So effectively had this campaign been carried out that by the winter of 1957-58 (little more than eight years after Liberation) cholera, small pox and typhus had been virtually exterminated and infant mortality greatly reduced. These results were achieved by sanitation measures and education in hygiene, by a large-scale program for training doctors, technicians and nurses, and by establishing hospitals, clinics and first-aid stations, sanitariums, rest homes and research centres.

A very important part of the campaign for better health consisted in getting people, old as well as young, to avail themselves of those cheapest and most abundant of all health aids: sunshine, fresh air, good water and physical exercise. To this end, life in the open,—hiking, bathing, camping, mountaineering, outdoor games and sports were encouraged. School children spent a part of each day exercising and playing games in the fresh air. Each day radio programs exhorted adults to do their daily dozen exercises outdoors or with open windows. To the accompaniment of radio music appropriate exercises were suggested and directed.

Our windows in Shanghai overlooked a large athletic field. All day long runners were trotting round the track, and tennis and basketball were being played. In gardens and green areas from dawn on we saw grey-beards and young people doing calisthenics on their own. If the People's Government has succeeded in nothing else, it has made the

173

Chinese health-conscious and provided the people with the incentives for achieving and maintaining good health.

Reform movements with which we have been dealing thus far were designed chiefly to transform the environment of the Chinese people from semi-feudal backwardness toward cooperative modern living. There was another reform of the very greatest importance,—a reform of the people themselves. It was desirable to build a socialist society. It was equally necessary to prepare people born and conditioned by the life of pre-Liberation China for the quite different life of socialist China.

Nationwide efforts to reform individual Chinese are described as the rectification movement. Rectification means making "right people" who will be prepared and eager to live in a "right" world. "Right," in this case, means "willing to take part in building socialism and to live peacefully and fraternally in a socialist community as it is being built." Success in all of the other campaigns depends to a great extent upon the effectiveness with which the individual is rectified, or set right.

Chinese people, individually, and in groups based on geography, language, nationality, ideology and other factors, face the task of co-existence today as well as tomorrow. Granted the Chinese people have agreed to build socialism, where do they find, or how do they propose to develop individuals who are willing and able to take on such a task and carry it to a successful conclusion?

The problem presents three aspects. The first is co-existence in a semi-feudal, semi-capitalist, semi-colonial country while socialism is being developed. The second aspect is the heart-breaking struggle to build a socialist sector in an antagonistic capitalist world. The third is to prepare individuals and social groups to survive and function in a socialist world once it is established.

Many socialists in the West are eager to change the world, but most of them express no great interest in changing themselves, or in developing human beings who are capable of building such a world and equally capable of living in it after it is built. Among those socialists who realize that it will take re-made human beings to live in a socialist world, and to function under the new conditions which are the pre-requisites of socialism, only a tiny minority are willing to make the requisite changes in their own pre-socialist way of life.

Our experience leads us to believe that the Chinese policy makers, more than any other group of socialists with whom we have been in contact, realize the importance of the problem and are willing to make the necessary adjustments in their own lives. Chinese people, like their fellow humans elsewhere, are not merely creatures of habit. They are also victims of traditions, customs, economic and social forces and pressures which shape and reshape them every day of their lives. Many of these traditions, customs, social forces and habits are deeply rooted in a capitalist past or even in a feudal past. Once established they not only persist but are perpetuated, often with dogmatic and fanatical zeal, by those who live more in the past than they do in the present.

Must we conclude from this analysis that the past dominates the present? That conclusion is inescapable, whether we deal with humanity, with society or with nature. Today the past reigns supreme. And tomorrow? In tomorrow lies the hope, because in the course of today it is possible for a self-conscious, rational, ingenious, imaginative, creative being to introduce new elements into today's pattern and by such innovations to shape the future in terms of his own visions, imaginings, pre-conceptions, plans and actions.

If this is true, human beings and human communities can lift themselves out of complex habit patterns and social opposites, and thus, in effect, renovate and rebuild both nature and society. The great contribution of socialism to human well-being and progress during the past century has been this awareness of the possibility that humanity can consciously and deliberately remake the natural and social environments. For many years this possibility existed largely in the realm of socialist theory. The practice of the past forty years, first in the Soviet Union and later in East Europe and Asia, gives factual and experimental support to the theory that man can utilize and conserve nature and can build a new social pattern according to plan.

People's China, or any other community which has turned its back on competition, exploitation, acquisition, accumulation and turned its face toward cooperation, mutual aid, coexistence, peace and friendship, must not only establish new relations with nature and society, but must produce women and men capable of building socialism and also capable of living as socialists.

During our travels we have met many people in the countries which are most successful with socialist construction. Invariably they have enthused about the greater social security and the improved educational and cultural opportunities. At the same time many of these enthusiasts referred half regretfully to some deviations from Western practices. "There's too much talk of discipline on the job," some have said. "Trade unions over-emphasize increased production. Should they not rather stress the class struggle?" "Why no night clubs? Should not a man be free to stay out all night if he wants to?" "But I am a poet! Would you send a poet to a backward village?"

There is a need for human beings reared in a capitalist environment to be reborn into socialism. This is expressed in the Western term re-naissance. Proselytizing religionists have sought to "convert" non-believers. Psychoanalysts aim to free individuals from inhibitions and frustrating complexes. Philosophers and teachers have held up ideals of truth, justice and beauty, urging their followers to turn from lesser goals and seek only the highest. The rectification movement in China contains something of all these elements, coupled with a note of urgency. "Unless we rectify ourselves and do it now, we can neither build socialism nor can we be fit to live in a socialist society."

Westerners observing People's China are handicapped by lives spent in a society agonizing in its fascist death-throes and are unable to understand fully the rectification campaign now taking place. In a sense it parallels the Reformation, the Renaissance and the Enlightenment which swept Europe between the 12th and 18th centuries. However, there is one essential difference. The Reformation, the Renaissance and the Enlightenment left the masses of Europe illiterate serfs or impoverished, exploited wage workers. It was a relatively small part of the population belonging to the expanding bourgeois world which enjoyed the chief benefits of the new bourgeois order.

In China, on the other hand, it is the land workers and those who do the work of industry, transport and commerce who are the chief beneficiaries of the new life. It is those who have lived in the poorest dwellings who are being assigned to the new living quarters. It is the children of the most impoverished who have received scholarships which guarantee them an education. As science and technology

177

come to the fore in socialist countries, scientists and those who have acquired technical competence are reaping rewards in recognition and material benefits in the form of higher living standards, better scientific equipment and greater scope for their experiments. But the real beneficiaries are the illiterate, impoverished, superstition-ridden, partly-employed masses that, until this generation, have continued to live in darkness and who now see light.

In the first instance, the rectification movement is directed at the "technological intelligentsia," against those who under present conditions might, through control of the state apparatus, become a new class of taskmasters and exploiters. It is this group that must be set right (rectified) and kept right. In a broad sense, however, the rectification campaign is directed against anyone and everyone who clings to bourgeois ideas and ideals, who, wittingly or unwittingly, is helping to restore capitalism in any form, or who is hindering socialist construction.

We discussed rectification with many Chinese. Among them was a young man recently graduated from a university. We asked him what he considered was the most important single factor in the present-day improvement of People's China. "The rectification movement," he replied.

"How far does this movement go?" we asked. "How many people are being reached by it?"

"Rectification is reaching everyone," he said, "from grandfathers to babes in arms."

"What is being rectified?" we questioned further.

"Every aspect of life: the tendency to aggression, to seek prestige and power for their own sake, subjectivism, sectarianism, burocracy."

"What means are being used to rectify?" we asked.

"We are avoiding denunciation and recrimination. We

refrain from name calling. We patiently point out mistakes, meeting argument with argument until we convince our rightists that their ideas are no longer applicable to the present conditions in People's China."

"Where is this rectification process going on?" we inquired.

"All over the country, in cities, towns and villages," was the answer. "We are using meetings, wall newspapers, heart-to-heart talks. We intend to reach all of the people who are not prepared to live in a socialist China."

Another Chinese with whom we discussed rectification was a Communist Party member with a long record of dedication to the cause. "Rectification," said he, "is one of the most significant steps we have taken in our long march to prepare the Chinese people to live in a socialist China. The movement was begun in April, 1957. It has four stages. Stage 1: A group of people gets together and everyone says what is on his mind. If anyone hesitates to speak, the others help. Stage 2: We come to grips with our central problem. Should People's China be socialist or capitalist? The Great Debate continues for weeks or months, with all taking part. Stage 3: We modify ideas, correct individual and organizational shortcomings and mistakes. In our group we are now in this third stage of rectification. Stage 4: the summing up. We review our discussions, try to find out what each has gained from rectification.

"To pass through such an experience is like leaping into a pool of cold water on a warm day. You come out feeling like a new person. Actually the rectification process turns out new people. Never again can we be the same people we were before the process began."

Rectification is going on in every organized group, all over People's China. Millions are passing through its successive stages. From self-criticism the individual learns to see himself and evaluate his thoughts and actions against the general purpose of building socialism. Through discussion self-criticisms are evaluated. Then come the steps for reform and a program of action which will help the individual who is being rectified to correct his past mistakes. Such a program is formulated with the assistance of the group. Finally there is the summary of conduct or practice over a period of time or in a particular situation. If this summary shows that the individual is not yet rectified, the process begins all over again and continues until rectification is completed to the satisfaction of the group concerned.* The group involved may be a primary trade union, an agricultural collective, the staff of a school, a residential committee, or any one of the many primary groups in which the peoples of China come together.

One of our Chinese associates who was deep in the rectification campaign summarized the situation thus: "This is the crucial movement in which the success or failure of our efforts to build socialism will be decided. It is relatively easy to change institutions. It is hard to modify traditions, to challenge customs, to stand up against social pressure, to alter habits, especially those that were established in early life. Failure in this effort would be tragic. Success, even in a moderate degree, will usher in a new day for China and for the world."

Rectification is penetrating every corner of People's China. It is too early to form any valid judgment as to its

* Case histories of rectified individuals and detailed descriptions of rectification techniques will be found in *Prisoners of Liberation*, N.Y.: Cameron Associates, 1957. Allyn and Adele Rickett, who spent several years in Chinese prisons and who were rectified in the main by their fellow prisoners, follow the process through its various stages until rectification is complete.

effect on the development and success of socialist construction. If it achieves its twin purposes of unifying theory and practice and preparing human beings born and reared in the Old World to live successfully in the New World, it will be one of China's most valuable contributions to the conscious improvement of society by society.

People in the West who go in for reforms of any kind are looked upon as queer or abnormal. Normal Westerners find it more comfortable to conform than to reform. Here we found a whole country rolling up its shirt-sleeves and attempting, collectively, to learn how to live a better life. We have never encountered such robust strength, such earthiness, such powers of endurance coupled with a seeming delicacy and fragility. We found in the Chinese people a sincere humility alongside an unshakeable confidence in their step by step accomplishment of whatever tasks they set themselves. We found humor and lightness, with a deep underlying gravity and purposefulness. We found contentment with sparse simple living against a background of ancient culture and refinement. And, paramount, we found a willingness to learn, to change, to adapt and "rectify," duplicated nowhere else on earth.

People's China, in the course of the past eight years, has attempted to clean out one abuse after another. Each reform campaign is preceded and accompanied by appeals which aim to prepare the public mind and to convince public opinion that the particular reform campaign which is being undertaken is in the interest of one or another of the groups which compose the Chinese masses. Thus social reform is part and parcel of the life pattern of present-day China.

8. BUILDING SOCIALISM STEP BY STEP

We began our report on People's China with a brief historical note which emphasized the unplanned, undirected disorder and turmoil which the Chinese people endured through an entire century. Few benefited by it. Most regretted and deplored it. Some struggled valiantly to replace disorder with order, and turmoil with justice and freedom under law.

Beginning with "China's Good Earth" we noted several specific areas in which the life of the Chinese people has been reformed and transformed since Liberation. Planned changes are still going on. Some of them have involved relations with nature. Others have modified the structure of society. Still others have dealt with the human being, or, as we say in the West, with the individual.

Needless to say, the planners, designers and builders of socialism in China, with its long and distinguished social history, are well aware that the distinctions between nature, society and humanity are quite arbitrary, and are made for simplicity in analysis and for convenience in planning and blue-printing. The Chinese know (none better) that nature is a whole, made up of inter-woven, inter-penetrating, interdependent parts. The same axiom holds for society and for humanity. No matter how much sub-division may be necessary in studying an organism, the student dare not lose sight of the unity which is the essential character of the organism-as-a-whole.

Nature, society and humanity are the products of change, variation, growth and, often, of evolution. Any innovation or intervention in terms of quantity or of quality throws the organism-as-a-whole off balance. Unless this imbalance is compensated, change, variation and growth, during the period subsequent to the intervention, will follow a course which differs from the pre-intervention course, in direct relation to the quantity and quality of the intervention.

These generalizations or axioms occupy an honored niche in the hall of learning known as China's cultural heritage or cultural history. Also they occupy a prominent place in the thinking of those Chinese who are chiefly responsible for building socialism in People's China.

It is the Chinese who are building socialism in China. The Chinese have a respect for the Russians which sometimes comes close to reverence. The help which the Russians gave during the critical months immediately after Liberation was so generous, so timely and so effective that the Chinese never tire of referring to "our Soviet brothers" or "our great socialist neighbor." The Chinese have studied the Soviet pattern carefully and have learned much from it. But they are thinkers in their own right. They face a peculiar historical situation with which they are dealing in accordance with their own cultural heritage, in view of their own considerable revolutionary experience of the last hundred years, and on the basis of their own keen judgment of present situations inside People's China and of the relations between China and the non-Chinese world.

We had several opportunities to talk with Chinese who play an influential part in shaping policy. It might be helpful to the understanding of Chinese developments to give a brief account of their approach to the building of a socialist China. Invariably they begin with the Russian Revolution of 1917, which they call the October Revolution. This event, the Chinese believe, inaugurated the era of the transformation of the old capitalist world into the new socialist world.

Since the October Revolution socialist construction has extended the frontiers of socialism far beyond the borders of the Soviet Union, until the socialist countries have 35 percent of the population, 25 percent of the land area and turn out a third of the industrial product of the planet. Chinese planners believe that today the socialist countries form a big united family, with the Soviet Union occupying the place of honor at the family table.

China's revolution and its program of construction are part and parcel of the movement which began with the October Revolution. Before October, 1917, revolutionary struggles in China got nowhere, they observe. After October, after the foundation of the Communist Party, and as a result of the assistance given to the Chinese by the world revolutionary movement headed by the Soviet Union, the Chinese people were able to bring their long and bitter struggle for liberation to a victorious conclusion in 1949. The theory on which the successful struggle of the Chinese people was founded is Marxism-Leninism.

When the Chinese People's Republic was established in October, 1949, the construction of socialism began. In 1952 when the First Five Year Plan was being organized, the task before the Chinese Communist Party and the Chinese people was to build China into a powerful, socialist, industrialized state during three five year plans that would extend from 1953 to 1967. The first step during this period was the transfer of the privately owned means of production from private to public ownership. This step in the main was completed by 1956. The second and the far more difficult step was the transformation of a backward agricultural community into an advanced socialist industrial state. This step will be achieved in from two to three five year plans. Only after this second step will People's China have a firm material basis on which to build a socialist system.

During this transition period the Chinese people are confronted by three problems of the greatest importance. The first is the construction of a socialist super-structure for Chinese society. The second is heading off and circumventing any attempt to restore capitalism. The third problem is the transformation of people so that they can live successfully and happily in a socialist society. The basic principle which must be followed in handling all three problems is gradual change by peaceful means. This formula relies upon voluntariness, mutual benefit and state aid as the forces that will lead the Chinese people toward socialism.

Within this planned transformation of Chinese society is the organizational pattern of democratic centralism,—a combination of a high degree of democracy with a high degree of centralization. "The unity of democracy and centralism, of freedom and discipline, of administrative means and the means of persuasion and education—these are the special features of such socialist democracy," we were told.

Chinese thinkers are convinced that Chinese socialism has its special character. Despite this fact, it is one segment of a world-wide front:—the construction of a socialist world which will embrace the entire human race. In this sense socialist construction in China is a continuation of the great October Revolution of 1917.

Marxism-Leninism, the present guide to Chinese thinking and action, is not static. Rather it grows and evolves with the broadening experience derived from the building of socialism. The transition to socialism in each country contributes to Marxism-Leninism and enriches it.

This sequence of ideas will be found in the pronouncements of the Chinese Communist Party and in the thinking of theorists and social engineers. It has been hammered out through the five decades of struggle that followed the Revolution of 1911 and especially during the period since the organization of the Chinese Communist Party. As elsewhere, there are differences in viewpoint and approach of the Chinese leaders to the theoretical and practical problems which they face, but these differences are of minor importance compared with the vast areas of agreement which Chinese leadership has attained and maintained. There seems to be far less factionalism in China than in Western left movements, and a greater determination to put first things first, establish a stable socialist economy and society and then, if anyone has the inclination, devote time and energy to hair-splitting and petty wrangling.

We found in China no trace of such millenial concepts as "God is in his heaven, all is right with the world," or, in contemporary language, "We have achieved socialism. At this point we have entered an earthly paradise, while a static nature contemplates our bliss and social history stands still." Their knowledge is based on practice rather than on authority. It might be more accurate to say that their technique is to test authority by practice, leaning rather heavily on a practice in which ingenuity and innovation are important elements.

Chinese socialists are the first to tell a visitor that building socialism is a process, a causal sequence or series which will continue until it reaches a new social level or synthesis and from that vantage point enters upon the next cycle of change, variation and growth. The central problem, as they see it, is to measure the forces at work, to understand their character and the principles or laws which govern their action, to restore or preserve balance, and where necessary to intervene by introducing new elements into the process.

186

No one among our many friends and acquaintances in People's China believes the problem can be handled by striking one final blow for peace and freedom or by taking this or that one gigantic leap into a static perfection, which will mark the end of the historical process. Rather, it is to work reasonably and wisely with the forces available in the given historical situation, and thus to proceed, step by step, toward the goals of socialism.

Perhaps we should introduce still another line of thinking in order to clarify for western minds the realistic or practical, but developmental, Chinese thinking. We heard no Chinese say: "We have reached socialism" with the same connotation that would surround the sentence "We have reached Shanghai." Socialism, in Chinese thinking (as we made contact with it), is neither a monolithic goal nor a circumscribed state of being. Rather it is a sequence or process of social change. Like "feudalism" or "capitalism," both of which evolved through centuries, socialism had its beginnings in social history. It is presently maturing and expanding. Its development will lift the human race (and particularly the masses of industrial and land workers) to higher levels of theory and practice, not only in the natural and social sciences and their application in natural and social engineering and technology, but perhaps more significantly in the realm of social awareness, social ethics and realized and activized responsibility for the planning, organization and administration of the body social.

According to the Bible story, Jehovah through his servant Moses, won his people independence from slavery under the Egyptian monarchy and led them across the Red Sea toward the Promised Land of Milk and Honey. After the Israelites had deviated several times from the Path of Righteousness, Jehovah lost patience, abandoned his efforts to save the liberated bond-slaves, and had Moses keep them in the desert for forty years until all of the ex-slaves (including their leader) were dead, and had been replaced by a new generation, born in freedom, which was ready to take over and inhabit the Promised Land.*

Chinese leaders, unlike Jehovah have not lost patience. On the contrary, they are filled with hope and confidence. They are leading a campaign to utilize and adapt nature, to rebuild society and to change human nature during the life of the present liberated generation. They propose to make the Promised Land of China support the population, reform the social pattern and meanwhile they are preparing humanity to live in the New World which all are helping to build. They propose to achieve these results, not with fairy wands or magic carpets, but by organizing all of the people, offering as much education as each can utilize, by calling for volunteers to deal with special difficulties and problems, and by analysis, argument and persuasion to keep the various and quite different elements of China's teeming population marching toward a classless, cooperative society based on peace, friendship and mutual respect both at home and abroad.

During the first decade after Liberation the Chinese have attempted to build socialism in four coordinated fields: the central plan; joint business enterprise; agricultural, industrial and trade cooperatives, and the widespread organization of popular movements based on the principle of democratic centralism.

Central planning speaks for itself. It requires theoretical clarity, practical experience and sufficient public support and administrative authority to put the plan into operation and

* Lincoln Steffens' *Moses in Red* presents an enlightening analysis of this episode.

carry it through to its conclusion. Central planning is chiefly a task for experts and specialists.

Beside the central plan there are local plans of two kinds. First, the local geographical plans of provinces, regions, counties and cities, made with general reference to the central plan but with a large measure of local autonomy. Second, local functional plans made by industries, transportation units, cultural institutions, trade and agricultural collectives. A factory or mine would fulfill its production; it would also provide for improvements, betterments and expansion of its facilities, or for increased quality of its product. Beside these technical advances it would construct housing and cultural facilities for its own workers and their families. An agricultural collective would improve production directly by seed selection or crop rotation. It would also improve buildings, dig wells, lay out roads, ponds, install pumps. Thus each geographical or functional unit under the general plan is activated into planning on its own behalf and for its own specific or general betterment.

Popular movements have played a particularly large role in China's advance toward socialism. Where there was a massive task in which manpower counted, people have been invited and encouraged to take part. Road and bridge building, construction of dikes and dams, and tree planting have been carried on by singing, chanting men and women, students and soldiers, government workers and farmers, volunteering their services, and organized and directed by competent engineers and administrators. By such means the earthworks for controlling the Huai River or the approaches to the Yangste Bridge were completed in record time and at minimal cost. When the jobs were done, hundreds of thousands or millions could point to the imposing result of joint enterprise and say, "We got together and did that job. I also had a hand in it."

Parts of this conception of building a new world of social-ism step by step are inherent in China's long cultural history. Other parts have developed out of the revolutionary experi-ences accumulated by the Chinese themselves since the Tai Ping Revolution of 1851-64. Still other parts have been gleaned by studying the history of Western capitalism and the theories and practices of Western revolutionaries and West-ern revolutions (particularly the October revolution in the Soviet Union) and Soviet experience with planning. These and other strands of knowledge and understanding are being spun and woven into the culture pattern which the observers and chroniclers of contemporary events are beginning to describe as the New China.

9. THE GOVERNMENT AND THE PEOPLE OF CHINA

We have referred to the leaders and the shapers of public policy in People's China. We have given some detail con-cerning the spectacular changes which have been brought about under their direction during the single decade since New China's Liberation. Also we have tried to pay our re-spects to the discernment, infinite patience and the deter-mined, persistent efforts which leaders and followers alike have brought to the herculean tasks of restoration and recon-struction in a country having the continental geographical area and vast population of China. The purposes have been noble, the conceptions splendid, the execution has been magnificent in scope and workmanlike in detail. The main objective (richer and more rewarding lives for all members of the human family, including the peole of China) has always been kept clearly in view.

These are strong words. This is high praise. We use the words advisedly and with a full sense of the responsibility which their use implies. We bestow the praise deliberately and gladly because our rather extensive reading about modern China and our visit to that country in the winter of 1957-58 have convinced us that the leaders, policy makers, planners and administrators of People's China have been (to themselves, somewhat unexpectedly, and to us, rather marvelously) successful in their efforts to transform a big, populous, ramshackle, disorganized, disintegrating community into a coordinated integrated going concern. Even more significantly, perhaps, they have achieved these noteworthy results largely through minutely detailed organization, and persuasion based on a reasoned appeal to the widespread human yearning for order, security, freedom and improvement.

How have such results been achieved? Broadly, through mature collective thinking, through detailed collective planning, through collective action meticulously organized on the broadest possible basis among the Chinese people. When the time came, the Chinese leaders stood up together, and they have been standing together and working together since Liberation. More than anything else it is the togetherness that seems to be the key to the successes of People's China during the critical first years of its existence. China, in very truth, is one big family.

Individuals like Chairman Mao Tse-tung and the Prime Minister, Chou En-lai, appear in public on state occasions and are quite accessible to those who have legitimate business with them. But Chinese leadership is collective in a very real sense. Questions are raised and issues are discussed thoroughly,—so thoroughly that the decisions and policies com-

191

mand all but unanimous support before they reach the level of public decision. In fact, the decisions grow out of the discussions.

Be sure of one thing. Matters concerning public policy are not "top secret" in China. On the contrary, they are discussed actively and openly, everywhere, any time, in season and out. Also, they are on the record, in print, for anyone to read, and may be found taking shape in public and private life all over China.

Legally, the nucleus of political life in People's China is the Constitution of 1954 and the governmental structure established in accordance with constitutional provisions. But the moving force in Chinese political life is the democratic united front,—the Chinese People's Political Consultative Conference, which "seeks to unite all nationalities, classes, political parties, mass organizations and notable public figures without party affiliation in China and over-seas Chinese" in a non-official body that represents all of the Chinese people. While the CPPCC has no political authority, it is composed of all political forces which are aiming at the establishment of socialism in China.

Nine political parties are the chief component elements in the CPPCC: the Communist Party, the Revolutionary Committee of the Kuomintang, the China Democratic League, the China Democratic National Construction Association, the China Association for Promoting Democracy, the Chinese Peasants and Workers Democratic Party, the Chinese Chi Kung Tang, the Chiu San Society and the Taiwan Democratic Self-Government League.

Theoretically each of the nine parties which are members of the CPPCC is autonomous and equal. Practically, the Communist Party is the leading group in the Chinese People's Political Consultative Conference. Each of the nine parties which are members of the CPPCC represents a tendency or trend that developed during the two decades 1927-49 when the final struggle for the control of China took place. Each has an agreed number of deputies in the National People's Congress (the National Parliament) and in the CPPCC. A majority of the members elected to the National People's Congress are also members of the Communist Party. Mao Tse-tung, who is chairman of the Communist Party, is Honorary Chairman of the CPPCC. Chou En-lai, who is a Vice Chairman of the Communist Party, is Chairman of the CPPCC.

The CPPCC works through a National Committe of which Mao Tse-tung is Honorary Chairman and Chou En-lai, Vice Chairman of the Communist Party, is Chairman. This committee holds meetings, hears and discusses reports and otherwise concerns itself with five tasks: " (1) In cooperation with the government, and by setting social forces in motion, to solve social problems arising out of the inter-relationship between different classes, to keep in close touch with the people at large, to bring their opinions and their suggestions to the notice of governmental bodies. (2) To solve by thorough consultation problems affecting cooperation within the CPPCC or between any of the different parties, groups or organizations affiliated to it. (3) To exchange views on international problems. (4) To exchange views on the nomination of candidates to the National Peoples Congress and local peoples congresses, and on the nominations of members of the political consultative congresses at all levels. And (5) to make arrangements for members to study Marxism-Leninism and to remould outworn ways of thinking on a voluntary basis." * Issues coming before the National Committee of the CPPCC are discussed until a concensus of opinion is reached.

* *Handbook on People's China,* pp. 97-98.

The issues are not decided by majority vote. Discussion continues until unanimity is achieved.

So far as we are aware, the CPPCC has no parallel in the political superstructure of any country other than People's China. Although it has no political authority, it is closely linked with public authority from the lowest to the highest levels.

The Communist Party is the moving force in the CPPCC. It is also the moving force in the Government of China. Mao-Tse-tung is Chairman of the Communist Party. He is also Chairman of the People's Republic of China. The Communist Party of China, founded July 1, 1921, is "the vanguard of the Chinese working class, the highest form of its class organization. Taking Marxism-Leninism as its guide to action, the Party aims at the achievement of socialism and communism in China." "The central task of the Party at the present time is to lead the Chinese people to transform China as soon as possible from a backward agricultural country into a socialist industrial country." The first significant step in this direction was taken in 1955 and 1956 when "the Party led the people to the over-all and decisive victory in the socialist transformation of agriculture, handicrafts and capitalist industry and commerce." * Membership in the Party has grown from 57 in 1921 and 950 in 1925, to 1,210,000 in 1945 and 12,720,000 in December, 1957.

Communist Party organs play a prominent role in initiating policies and directing them toward the immediate Party objective—a socialist and communist China. In order to carry out these tasks, the Party is organized to function at all levels in all of the organs that are authorized to initiate public policies and carry them into effect.

The Communist Party is part of a sequence which begins

---

* *Handbook on People's China,* pp. 85-86.

with the Pioneers in the elementary school and continues through the Youth League at the middle school and college level until it reaches the Communist Party at adulthood. At all levels the aim is to get into the organization the most able, gifted and competent elements, and prepare them to lead the popular movement for a socialist and communist People's China.

Theoretically the Communist Party of China is the vanguard of the industrial and land workers and is leading the Chinese people toward socialism and communism. In order to achieve this result, the Party works in a democratic united front whose constituent elements (the nine parties of the CPPCC) and whose organ of united action, the CPPCC, agree on one main objective,—a socialist China.

During 1949 the People's Liberation Army captured Nanking, the seat of the Kuomintang Government. In the course of that year, the process of liberating the Chinese mainland was virtually completed. In September the Communist Party, together with the other political parties which had cooperated in the grim days of the struggle for national liberation and democracy, called in Peking the Chinese People's Political Consultative Congress. On October 1, 1949, Chairman Mao Tse-tung, speaking in the name of the CPPCC, proclaimed the founding of the People's Republic of China.

China's public business was transacted by the Central People's Government Council acting for the CPPCC from October, 1949, until September, 1954. Meanwhile, in January, 1953, a Committee for Drafting the Constitution, headed by Chairman Mao Tse-tung, was formed by the Central People's Government Council. In March, 1954, this committee accepted the first draft of the Constitution submitted by the Central Committee of the Communist Party of China. Discussions of this first draft extended over two months. Meet-

195

ings were held in Peking and the other principal cities of China. Members of the National Committee of the CPPCC, spokesmen of the various political parties, for the people's organizations, and for all sections of society took part in the discussions.

From these discussions a revised draft of the Constitution emerged, was accepted by the Central Government People's Council on June 14, 1954, was printed in millions of copies and translated into the Mongolian, Tibetan, Iughur, Kazakh and Korean languages. Then for three months the draft constitution was discussed at meetings in which an estimated 150 million people from all sections of China took part. During this nation-wide discussion, suggestions for amendments and revisions were made and were considered by the Committee for Drafting the Constitution. After further revisions, the draft constitution was adopted by the Committee for Drafting the Constitution, and submitted to the Central People's Government Council on Sept. 9, 1954. When the First National People's Congress met on Sept. 15, 1954, the final draft of the Constitution was submitted and after discussion was adopted on September 20, 1954.

The Constitution contains a Preamble, a first chapter of general principles, a second chapter describing the state structure, and a third chapter on the fundamental rights and duties of citizens.

Under the Constitution, the People's Republic of China is a people's democratic state led by the working class and based on the worker-peasant alliance. The preamble states that a broad people's democratic front, led by the Communist Party and composed of all democratic classes, political parties and people's organizations, will continue to rally the people of China for the fundamental tasks specified in the Constitution during the transition to socialism.

Transition to socialism is to be effected by the organs of the state, by social forces, including socialist industrialization and socialist transformation, which will insure the gradual abolition of exploitation and the building of a socialist society. Under the Constitution, all power belongs to the people and is to be exercised through the National People's Congress and the local people's congresses. All state organs are to maintain close contact with the people and to work under popular supervision. Citizens may bring charges against any government worker for violation of law or for neglect of duty.

Many freedoms and rights are specified in the third chapter of the Constitution, such as the right to vote and to stand for election, freedom of speech, of the press, of assembly, of association, procession and demonstration, and freedom of religious belief. Freedom of the person and homes of citizens is inviolable, and privacy of correspondence is assured. All citizens are guaranteed the right to work and to education, to rest and to leisure and to material assistance in old age, sickness or disability. Women have equal rights with men in all spheres,—political, economic, social and domestic. The state protects marriage, the family, mothers and children. The Constitution also provides for state protection of lawfully earned incomes, savings, houses and other means of livelihood as well as the right to inherit private property according to law.

All citizens, under the Constitution, must abide by the Constitution and the law, uphold discipline at work, keep public order and respect social ethics. Citizens must respect and protect public property, pay taxes and perform military service.

All nationalities in China are united "in one great family of free and equal nations." Discrimination is prohibited, as

197

is any act that will disturb the unity of the nationalities. Each nationality is guaranteed the right to use its own language and to determine its own customs and habits. All national minorities living together in compact communities in given areas have the right to regional autonomy.

International relations, under the Constitution, must be directed toward world peace and the progress of humanity. China will foster the established friendship with the Soviet Union, with the People's Democracies and with all peace-loving people throughout the world. The Chinese Government will establish and maintain diplomatic relations with all countries on the basis of equality, mutual benefit, mutual respect for each other's sovereignty and territorial integrity.

Under the Constitution the National People's Congress is the supreme organ of legislative and executive power. It also elects the President of the Supreme People's Court and the Chief Procurator of the Supreme People's Procuracy and has authority to remove any of its appointees from office. Through its standing committees, its officers, its State Council and the ministries and commissions under the State Council, the public life of the Chinese People's Republic is directed step by step toward socialism.

Present-day China is something more than a big family. It is an organized family. Practically everyone in China belongs to one or more organizations. Take an agricultural village as an example. Everyone in the village is a citizen of the township, with its officials corresponding to those in an American village. It is their business to see that civic obligations are carried out and rights are respected. In addition to these representatives of the village or township who are "public officials" in the American sense of that term, most individuals and families are part of a cooperative with well-defined responsibilities and rights in that organization. About

198

97 percent of China's land workers are members of cooperatives. Members of the Communist Party, of the Youth League and of the Young Pioneers belong to their respective local organizations and take an active part in village affairs. Beside these more or less official organizations, there are unofficial or private bodies dealing with education, health, peace and any other matters of general concern.

Towns or cities are similarly organized, but in a slightly different way. The primary geographical group is the residential or block committee, working closely with the Women's League, the Communist Party, the Youth League and the Pioneers. Children are organized in their classes, their schools and their recreation. One of the most important organizations in town and city is the trade union network, which includes about 95 percent of China's wage workers. Consumer cooperatives, trade cooperatives, school committees and peace committees cover other aspects of organizational life.

Cooperatives of various sorts have a long history in China, but the present-day cooperative movements have expanded with explosive suddenness in the years since Liberation. The largest and most widespread cooperative network is that of agriculture. Land reform left the individual peasant with one or more personally-owned plots. Because of the very limited amount of fertile land per head of China's rural population, most of these holdings were insufficient in size to provide more than a bare living for the farm family, even when the able-bodied members of the household spent their spare time in working out for wages.

Before 1949, land workers in the liberated areas had begun to form mutual aid teams, some of which were on a seasonal basis and some on a year-round and fairly permanent basis. Half a dozen households made up these teams. Each house-

199

hold owned its land. There was little common ownership of animals or implements. These mutual aid teams justified themselves by raising per acre productivity, especially on land farmed by the year-round mutual aid groups. Households engaged in mutual aid teams were capitalist insofar as they owned the land and worked it for profit. They were socialist insofar as they had abandoned competition and adopted mutual aid.

Producers cooperatives began replacing mutual aid teams immediately after Liberation. The early cooperatives were made up of from 20 to 50 households. The economy was a mixture of common and private property in land, implements and animals. In December, 1953, the Communist Party decided to speed up the growth of agricultural cooperatives in order to keep pace with the rapidly expanding socialist industrial economy. Early in 1954 there were 58,000 agricultural producer cooperatives. By the middle of 1954, two-thirds of all peasant households belonged to mutual aid teams or producers cooperatives. In July, 1955, there were 650,000 cooperatives with 17 million members. During the next year the number of cooperatives increased to around a million, embracing 110 million households.

Within a decade the Chinese countryside has passed through two revolutions. The first was land reform. The second enrolled 95 percent of China's rural households in collective farms with no private property in land, animals or implements. Some disturbances accompanied the first of these revolutions. The second, already in its final stages, has been almost entirely peaceful, and by persuasion and example.

China's countryside decided to go socialist in the two or three years beginning with 1953. This decision was made in the last analysis by the land workers themselves. But in the ceaseless debate which preceded this final decision, members

200

of the Communist Party played an important role. The Party had nearly 4 million rural members early in 1955 and well over 7 million in 1956.

Agricultural reform and revolution have been important factors determining the direction of China's domestic policy in the years immediately preceding and following 1949. Industrial workers supported socialist construction before the First Five Year Plan was adopted in 1953. By 1955 the rapid development of cooperatives had tipped the balance of People's China toward socialism.

Residential or block committees are one of the basic organizations in Chinese towns and cities. If a new campaign is launched or if a new policy is adopted, the purposes of the campaign or the policy are explained to the people by the responsible elected leaders of the primary organizations, the residential committee, the Communist Party local, the Youth League local, the trade union local, or the local of the Women's League.

The chairman of a Block Committee was explaining the workings of this residential organization to us. Said he, "I may be called on the telephone or otherwise contacted and asked to explain some new development or policy. If the matter is urgent, within half an hour we can reach every householder in our block organization. Each one will be told what is proposed, why it is proposed and what each person is expected to do to carry out the proposed action. This is done not only by notices posted and handbills distributed, but by neighbors, speaking to each other—mouth to ear."

This block chairman was a pedicab driver. He was a member of a cab cooperative. Two men worked one pedicab in shifts. His position as Block Chairman took a considerable amount of his free time. This time he contributed as his share of "social work" (work for the general welfare). He was a small, quiet, simple man, but quite vocal. He talked smilingly and confidently about the duties and responsibilities of a block committee and a block chairman as neighbors crowded into the tiny Block Committee office where we were sitting on low, home-made benches. Children came and went. People crowded the open doorway of the office and poked their heads in the windows.

Beside the chairman, on the same bench, sat the vice-chairman, a jovial, middle-aged, black-haired mother of three, who was also chairman of the block women's committee. Like the chairman, this woman joined easily in the conversation, discussed block problems and told of the improvement in local living conditions since Liberation, with special emphasis on the complete change which Liberation had made in the status of women.

On rude wooden benches, in a small room, in one of the poorest quarters of Shanghai, we sat around a low table with cups of Chinese tea in front of us and talked about the problems and the future of People's China. We were two travelers from foreign parts, with an interpreter friend. They were two of the leaders,—policy makers and administrators of present-day China,—a pedicab driver and a neighborhood housewife. The people of the neighborhood within hearing distance (and they were crowded all around the little office) closely followed every phase of the discussion. Interest in New China and its problems seemed to be as keen in the primary organizations as it was toward the top of the prestige-power pyramid.

Among the important people's organizations are the trade unions which have developed with the expansion of industry, transportation and commerce. By the end of 1957, when the Eighth All China Trade Union Conference was held in Peking, membership in the 22 industrial union departments which compose the All China Federation of Trade Unions had passed the 16 million mark.

The All China Federation of Trade Unions, formerly called the All China Federation of Labor, was founded in 1925. After a checkered career, partly legal and partly underground, the Federation was given legal status by the Trade Union Law of 1950. The law provided for the basic interests of the working people and defined the function of trade unions, thus making the organized labor movement an organic part of People's China.

Chinese trade unions perform three chief functions. Their first task is to increase production by disciplined work, properly organized, by full use of technical facilities and technical knowledge and socialist competition and other devices to deepen the interest of the workers in establishing, reaching and exceeding production norms under an economic plan. Under a stable, socialist economy, increasing standards of living for the workers are possible as a consequence of heightened levels of production.

Second among trade union tasks is safeguarding and improving working conditions, safeguarding against accidents, reducing industrial health hazards and administering the system of social security applicable to workers.

The third task of the trade unions is to raise the cultural level of their members by providing facilities for housing, health, education and recreation.

Trade union organizations are directly responsible for the physical, economic, social and cultural well-being of their members. They are partly responsible for the successful development of an economic base upon which People's China can build socialism.

Other groups of people's organizations are those of youth,—the New Democratic Youth League of China, the All

China Federation of Democratic Youth and the All China Student Federation. The New Democratic Youth League is a mass organization of progressive youth, led by the Communist Party. In June, 1956, the League had 700,000 branches with a total membership of 20 million. One of the chief tasks of the League is the guidance of the Young Pioneers of China. The All China Federation of Democratic Youth, established in 1949, aims to unite all of the youth groups in China to build socialism at home and to establish and maintain unity and peace at home and abroad. The All China Federation is composed of 227 student organizations with 400,000 members.

During the whole of the present century, the youth of China have played a prominent role in the struggle to free China and Asia from the imperialists and to liberate the country from those elements in China which were in league with the imperialists. Today the youth are providing much of the energy and enthusiasm which are going into the building of a socialist China.

Women have played a decisive role in the struggle for Chinese liberation. Today they occupy responsible positions in every field of activity. Among the primary organizations throughout China, in the countryside as in the cities, are the women's organizations. Local, district and provincial organizations of democratic women are federated in the All China Women's Federation.

Other people's organizations deal with peace, with social welfare, with literature and art, with sport, with science and technology, with foreign affairs, with cultural interchange between People's China and foreign countries.

Formally, political parties and the agencies of government have been responsible for the transformation of People's China during the past decade. In another and a larger sense it is the people of China who have stood up and have taken the first steps toward cooperation, mutual aid, coexistence, peace and friendship. Without this popular fervor and popular enthusiasm, Liberation and socialist construction would have been far less complete, and perhaps impossible.

Wherever we went in People's China we found organization. Again and again the picture was reproduced: elected officials, men and women, young people and children at their posts of duty, keenly aware of their rights and the rights of their constituents, conscious of their responsibilities and of the importance to local, regional, provincial and national bodies that the rights be respected and the responsibilities be faithfully and efficiently fulfilled. We saw hundreds of such leaders, of all ages, during our stay in China. As far as we could learn, there were hundreds of thousands (perhaps millions) that we did not see, confidently and effectively carrying out their assignments.

Are you surprised, as we were, that block committees, agricultural cooperatives, trade union locals and women's committees should be staffed with so many elected officials, serving generally without pay, and doing their part conscientiously to build socialist China? Where did they come from? From all levels of the community. How were they trained? Many were taught in school, but most learned during the years of struggle preceding Liberation. Whether school-trained or educated by the hard battle for survival and improvement, all seemed to have learned two simple lessons. The first was that they must stand up before they could hope to go forward. The second was that they must all stand together and advance together toward their agreed objectives.

Who has been responsible for the miraculous transformation of People's China during the years since Liberation? We summarize our answer thus: The Chinese people under the leadership of a number of organizations, among which the Communist Party holds first place, are the Wonder Workers. Although they have had some sorely-needed help and advice from abroad, especially from the Soviet Union, it remains true that the development of People's China during the decisive decade beginning with 1949 is the work of the Chinese people themselves.

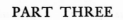

PART THREE

"Wherever a person travels, friends await his coming. In every land live the friendly, the kind, the good."

Chinese ballad singer

1. PEACEFUL SOCIALIST GIANTS

This book deals with two immense countries,—the Soviet Union and People's China. The first is geographically extensive, stretching east and west across two continents,—with almost three times the square mileage of the United States. The other country, somewhat larger than the United States, has nearly four times its population. The Soviet Union is gigantic geographically; People's China is gigantic demographically.

Among the dozen nations that are busy with various aspects of socialist construction, the Soviet Union and People's China occupy a distinctive position. They do so not only because of their vast geographical areas and their large populations, but chiefly because of the many important steps that each has taken in the direction of socialism,—steps made possible, at least in part, by their great geographical spaces and the diversity of their many peoples.

China and the Soviet Union are close neighbors, with long common frontiers. Both are attempting to build a socialist society that will equal and eventually excel and replace capitalism. But the two countries are unequally developed, economically and socially, and they occupy different positions in the time scale of modern history. The Soviet Union began building socialism in 1917, toward the end of the war of 1914-18. People's China turned to socialist construction thirty years later, after the end of the war of 1939-45. The Soviet Union therefore had an advantage of almost a generation over People's China in working out socialist construction techniques.

209

Traditionally and historically, major powers in close proximity have been rivals. At best their alliances have been uneasy and temporary, because each power was pursuing the ancient grab-and-keep, dog-eat-dog formula which has been at the basis of great power relationships for at least six thousand years of human culture history. The competitive grab-and-keep formula has been so deeply embedded in Eurasian relations for the last twenty centuries that it is almost impossible for a Westerner, trained in this tough school, to visualize any relationship between adjacent and relatively equal powers other than rivalry, intrigue, perfidy, treachery and war.

Consequently, when the Chinese People's Republic was proclaimed in October, 1949, Western observers, policy-makers and scholars took it for granted that the Soviet Union, which had inaugurated and in a sense pre-empted socialist construction, would attempt to humiliate, dominate and ultimately gobble up People's China, unless the latter, animated by the same power-grabbing impulse, became strong enough to subordinate and absorb the Soviet Union. Terms like "Soviet imperialism" and "communist imperialism" were coined and used to describe the process whereby each of these huge powers might be expected to expand into neighboring territory and establish its control over the neighboring people. Each step in their relations with one another was hailed as the beginning of imperialist grab-and-keep.

Both Russia and China have had similar experiences. Both have been through costly and disastrous wars. Both have endured the horrors of civil war. The people of both countries are weary of war and ardently desirous of peace. Foreign visitors to the Soviet Union and People's China during the past few years have brought back varied and often conflicting reports of conditions in the two countries. On one theme, however, the visitors have been in agreement: the people in these countries are desperately tired of war and are all in favor of peace.

After traveling about both countries in the winter of 1957-58 we are glad to verify this widely-reported observation. We were part of a delegation from the World Council of Peace to the November celebrations. In that capacity, we met many women and men who were devoting time and energy to the struggle against war. As a matter of course the question of war and peace was raised and discussed wherever we went. Without a single exception, the people with whom we talked were unreservedly and ardently for peace.

Naturally enough, members and associates of the peace councils, which are to be found all over the Soviet Union and People's China, were in favor of peace. Otherwise they would not have been contributing their time and energies to peace work. But we heard similar pro-peace sentiments from people who had no connection with peace organizations. In country and city, among workers, students, farmers, intellectuals, among soldiers and sailors, among women, men and children we found an abundance of pro-peace sentiment but no pro-war sentiment. Russians and Chinese of all shades of opinion and of widely differing professional backgrounds took their stand against war and in favor of peace.

Stalingrad was utterly destroyed during the 1942-43 battle for the control of the city. Of the many European and Asian cities that were damaged in the course of the savage 1939-45 conflict, none was so completely ruined as Stalingrad. No sooner had the invaders been driven out, than the Stalingrad people moved back into the ruins to clear away the debris, plan and rebuild. As a first part of their plan, the rebuilders of Stalingrad laid out one central street and built around it. Various names were suggested for this first street in the re-

211

born city. They did not call it Lenin Street, or Stalin or Gorki Avenue. By acclamation a name was selected: Peace Street. The choice bespoke the deepest desire of a people who had suffered so terribly from war that the interest which overtopped all others was their interest in peace.

There was another indication of the people's yearning for peace and their willingness to stand up and be counted. During the campaign to circulate the Stockholm petition against the use of atomic weapons, and during subsequent petition campaigns favoring peace, names were collected by the millions in both the Soviet Union and the Chinese People's Republic.

The pro-peace attitude of the people of the Soviet Union and People's China is not based on fear of war but on confidence in their theory and way of life. One Soviet trade unionist put the matter to us in this way. "We are not afraid of war. We have been through it and we have survived its cruelties and horrors. We know that we can take it. Just because we have been through it and suffered from it, we know how terrible war is. It wastes materials, but worse than that, it squanders human idealism, energy, wealth and life. Still worse, those of us who are trying to build a socialist society are diverted and preoccupied by war. We know from bitter experience that if we are to engage in socialist construction we cannot fight wars. War is a full-time occupation. Socialist construction is equally demanding. It is impossible to do both at the same time. There are many arguments against war. We present and support all of them. But for us who are striving in the face of formidable difficulties to build socialism, war is the last word in folly, because when war begins socialist construction not only stops, but the handiwork of a whole generation of socialist builders may be wiped out in one battle, as in the case of Stalingrad."

We travelled by train from Peking to Nanking with a Chinese officer who had been in the Fourth Liberation Army. He said to us, "We have had war enough and to spare. We have had war against the Japanese invaders and civil war among ourselves. Each was worse than the other. The time has come to end war and to make peace. Traditionally, we Chinese are a peaceful people. That would be enough in itself to line us up against war. But our generation has gone through the fires of war and we know its cost. We want no more of it. Much more important is the task to which we have been devoting ourselves since Liberation in 1949,—the building of a socialist China. If we are to succeed in establishing socialism, we *must* have peace.

"There's another point of great importance," he continued. "A score of Asian nations have won their independence from the Western empires during the past few years. All of them are trying to build up their countries. War, anywhere in Asia or in the world, upsets their economies and threatens their newly-won independence. We learned that lesson during the Korean War, which was only a passing incident in the lives of the Western powers. It came less than a year after our Liberation. It threatened us with another invasion. War in Korea forced us to postpone socialist construction for years. It was only after that war ended that we could launch our First Five Year Plan, in 1953."

During the summer of 1957 a Chinese who had graduated from the Massachusetts Institute of Technology in the United States was visiting Sochi, on the Black Sea, as a member of a tourist party from People's China. While there he chanced to meet a group of United States educators and officials who were touring the Soviet Union. At the request of the Americans, the Chinese tourist discussed with them the Chinese attitude toward world problems. Said he, "What we want more than anything else is peace. We need peace. If anybody doubts this he does not know China. Only with peace can we develop our country." *

These episodes illustrate a point of view which we encountered each time the issue of war and peace was discussed, by Russians or by Chinese. In every walk of life the people are opposed to war and ardently in favor of peace. Nor are they satisfied with verbal expressions and assurances of their horror of war and their longing for peace. They are organizing, agitating and building public sentiment in favor of replacing the cold war by cultural exchanges between peoples. They desire peaceful coexistence during the interim period when the governments are negotiating a comprehensive settlement.

We have called Part III of this book "Socialism, Peace and Friendship" because we believe that socialism, peace and friendship are closely related, interdependent ideas. Countries attempting to build socialism have a vested interest in establishing and maintaining peace, because unless they are able to devote their resources and energies to the multiple tasks of socialist construction they will hardly reach the goal of socialism.

For more than a century, socialist thinkers and organizers have held to this position. In its earliest stages socialist doctrine denounced the wastefulness of competition, proclaimed the destructive nature of militarism and war, described military preparations and military conflicts as "the highest form of capitalist competition" and advocated socialist cooperation as the only reliable guarantee of peace and friendship among the peoples.

Five decades of 20th century history have proved the correctness of the socialist contention that the competitive

* The Churchman, February, 1958, pp. 12-13.

214

struggle for wealth and power to which capitalist imperialism had devoted its major energies throughout the 19th century must eventuate, at the highest level, in a military conflict that would destroy the competitors. This, in a sentence, summarizes the history of 1910-58.

Half a century of destruction, disorganization and disintegration have brought to an inglorious end the epoch of capitalist imperialsm. The capitalists have had their say and their day. For all practical purposes, they have committed social suicide.

Social revolution in Russia, with its socialization of the means of production, its planned economy and cooperative society, its emphasis on science, technology and free public education, inaugurated a new epoch, the age of socialism, and placed the socialists and the socialists movement in the center of the world stage. Could socialism equal and excel capitalism in providing the necessaries and decencies of life for the human family? Could it, at the same time that it ended poverty and insecurity, establish peace and friendship among the peoples?

These questions will be answered definitely during the next three or four generations. In the meantime the socialist giants, and the less prominent nations and peoples which are attempting to build socialism, are having a chance to fulfill by their deeds the peace promises made by the socialists.

Specifically, the Soviet Union and People's China have had a decade during which to convert theory into practice and prove to the world that peace, mutual aid and friendship are aspects of the normal relationship between socialist neighbors.

Socialist countries, whether they are strong or weak, are engaged in the positive task of building socialism. It seems that there is a close connection between socialism and peace.

Without peace, no socialism. With socialism, there may be peace. Relations between the Soviet Union and People's China since 1949 provide evidence in support of this proposition.

2. SOVIET AID TO PEOPLE'S CHINA

People's China had the sympathy of the erstwhile colonial areas of Asia and Africa when it began building an industrialized, socialist society. It had the active support of the Soviet Union, and, to an increasing extent, of the European People's Democracies. Sympathy and token backing were cordially welcomed by the Peking Government. It was Soviet aid, however, which carried People's China through the five critical years, 1949-53, and made it possible for the Chinese to inaugurate their Five Year Plan at the beginning of 1953.

Among the chief powers, People's China could rely for whole-hearted backing only on the Soviet Union. India, which remained friendly but on the whole neutral, was also starting planned production, but instead of being in a position to give material assistance to China was itself in great need of outside economic aid. During the critical years that followed its establishment in 1949, People's China needed not neutrality but trained manpower, materials, machines and money. The Soviet Union furnished all four.

Soviet aid to People's China took several forms: a treaty of alliance; backing in the United Nations; loans; technical assistance. All four forms of aid were of the utmost importance to the newly organized government.

Soviet support in the United Nations was important but not crucial in China's development. Admission to the United Nations would have been of real help in stabilizing China's

216

international position. But the Soviet Union could not muster enough votes to secure China's admission or to prevent the passage of the United States' supported resolution declaring People's China aggressor in the Korean struggle.

Soviet loans of $300 million in 1950 and of 520 million rubles in 1954 were spent chiefly on capital goods. The first loan was made at one percent interest. Subsequent loans were at a slightly higher rate. The loans accounted for two or three percent of Peking's annual income.

Soviet technical aid was of profound importance in enabling People's China to reorganize its economy and to launch its First Five Year Plan in January, 1953. Trained manpower, experienced in industrial techniques, was woefully deficient in People's China. The Soviet Union met this need by sending Soviet personnel into China and by training Chinese personnel at home and in the Soviet Union. Thanks to its emphasis on the development of specialists and experts, by 1950 the Soviet Union had available numbers of scientists, engineers and technicians that could be loaned, at least temporarily, to a neighboring country which was proposing to build socialism. As soon as relations between Moscow and Peking were stabilized, the movement of Soviet specialists to China got under way.

Specialists in agriculture, conservation, industry, electronics, construction, moved eastward from Russia in a steady stream. Usually they went for periods of one or two years. As the first to go completed their tours of duty and returned to the Soviet Union, others took their places, so that for four or five years processions of Soviet experts were moving from the Soviet Union to People's China and from People's China back to the Soviet Union. The largest number of Soviet specialists in China at any one time has been estimated at 20,000.

217

Special hotels and other living quarters were provided for the Russian visitors. The largest of these, Friendship Hotel, was specially constructed on the outskirts of Peking for foreign specialists and their families. In every city we visited in China in the winter of 1957-58 we met these Russians, living in groups, with their borscht, caviar, black bread and sour milk and cream. Always they were unobtrusive, well-mannered, unassuming, business-like. Everywhere the comment on them was the same: "Our friends from the Soviet Union are our most valued and honored guests."

While we were visiting the great iron and steel complex in Anshan, North East China, we learned from the chairman of the plant's Trade Union Congress something about the effects of Soviet aid on North East China. "This enterprise was organized by the Japanese," he told us. "From the beginning the Japanese ran the plant. We Chinese were workers. We were not allowed to learn anything concerning formulas, processes, administration. All such know-how was for the Japanese and for them alone. Consequently, when the Japanese surrendered and left the plant, it was a body without a head. Then the Soviet Union came to our aid with materials, equipment and the much needed trained personnel. With this help we restored the plant and by 1952 we got it back into working order.

"The Soviet comrades were wonderful teachers," the chairman told us. "We were ready and eager to learn and they were equally ready to teach. Unlike the Japanese, who had told us Chinese nothing, the Soviet specialists stood at our elbows day and night, suggesting, guiding, directing. There were many of them here when we began production in 1952. Today there are only a few remaining. Those few will leave the plant during 1958 and return to the Soviet Union. After that, when we need special help, they will send the necessary

218

personnel to discuss new and difficult problems. They have no desire to take over our industry. Never have they tried to push us around. They have been generous teachers. We are grateful pupils. Now that we have mastered our tasks and are on our own, they are going to other places where they can continue to contribute their skills and their experience."

China's First Five Year Plan provided for 694 major projects. Soviet aid went to 156 of these projects, which were designed to provide Chinese economy with a coordinated foundation of "parent enterprises." Among them were 7 iron and steel mills, 27 power plants, 27 coal mines and coal-washing plants, and many engineering works. Of these 156 projects, 60 were in operation by the end of 1957; 70 were being built and the remaining 26 were in various stages of preparation.

Peng Min, director of the Yangtse River Bridge Engineering Bureau, told a story of personal friendship that illustrates and highlights Soviet technical aid to China. The Yangtse bridge, opened on October 1, 1957, was one of the major projects of the First Five Year Plan. Konstantin S. Silin, a Soviet engineer who had specialized in bridge construction, headed the group of Soviet experts that helped build the bridge.

Peng Min had worked with Silin on two previous bridge jobs, so they were old friends and knew each other's talents and peculiarities. When the Ministry of Railways assigned to Peng Min the responsibility for directing the Yangtse bridge job, he, Silin and the other Chinese and Soviet engineers drew up a construction program. The Yangtse was a deep river, 130 feet at flood level and nearly a mile wide at the point selected for the bridge. High water lasted for nine months of the year. Nine piers were to carry the bridge. If caissons were used, workers would be under a dangerous pressure of four atmospheres and would require special training and equipment which was not easily available. Even under the best of conditions caisson work would be slow and hazardous.

After going over the whole project carefully, Engineer Silin suggested that instead of caissons, they take five foot steel pipes, drive them into the mud on the river bottom, use mining drills inside the pipe to drill a hole into the rock, drive the pipe home with a special pile driver, pump out the water, put a steel reinforcing structure inside the pipe and fill the whole with concrete. A group of such pipes would serve as the anchor and core around which each pier would be built.

Necessary tools were constructed, the pipes were anchored into the rock and around them the piers were put in place. This method, never before used in bridge-building, took two years off the time necessary to finish the bridge. Instead of being opened some time in 1959, the bridge was ready for traffic on October 1, 1957, twenty-six months after the construction was begun.

"At the start of our work on the Yangtse Bridge," Peng Min wrote, "Silin and I had made a pact that he should pass on to me and the other comrades, all the time the job was going on, his knowledge of bridge building. And oh, what a lot we have learned! Silin is my friend and teacher. The nine years of our acquaintance and the three occasions on which we worked together, will live in my memory forever." *

Peng Min's autobiographical fragment goes to the heart of the relationship that grew up during the development of projects in all parts of China. The Soviet and Chinese specialists were comrades, working together to make a success of

* *People's China,* October 16, 1957. Hsu Pao-ting, deputy director of the Chinese Heavy Industry Bureau of the State Construction Commission, prepared an article for *China Reconstructs,* November, 1957, giving details of Soviet technical aid to China during the First Five Year Plan. Solomon Adler in *The Chinese Economy* devotes several pages to the question.

China's ambitious Five Year Plan. They bore another and very significant relationship to one another. Soviet specialists, with four decades of experience behind them, were the teachers. The Chinese, new at the work of building socialism, were the pupils. The teachers passed on what they knew to their pupils. The latter (already trained specialists in their own right) absorbed the new knowledge offered to them and tested it out on enterprises under joint teacher-pupil direction. Thus fortified with new experiences in theory and practice, the pupils were prepared to proceed on their own.

Aside from direct assistance in planning and equipping key units of the Chinese economy, the Soviet Union supplied gasoline, special steels, metal-cutting machinery, automotive units and other equipment. Plants constructed during the early stages of Soviet-Chinese collaboration were built largely to Soviet design and supplied with Soviet-made equipment. As Chinese plants expanded the production of capital goods, Chinese equipment was installed to a greater and greater degree. By the end of the Five Year Plan, new power stations, factories, and transport installations were largely, or, in some cases, wholly equipped with units made in China. In return for this aid, China sent the Soviet Union farm products, animal products, minerals and the products of light industry. Sino-Soviet trade was about five times as great at the end of 1957 as it had been in 1950.

While Soviet specialists were planning, directing and training in People's China, large numbers of Chinese (workers, technicians and students) went to the Soviet Union, to work in the industries, to take special training courses and, in the case of students, to enroll in Soviet higher schools. In the Soviet higher educational institutions we visited, we often saw Chinese students. Always the Russian comment concerning them was the same: "The Chinese are model students, hard-working and above reproach."

While we were in China many Soviet experts were returning to Russia. Only a few were being replaced. There were still highly technical jobs on which the Chinese were glad to have the advice and cooperation of Soviet specialists, but the bulk of the advisory and directing work had been done. We visited a number of enterprises in which Soviet experts had played an important part: in some plants, no Soviet personnel remained; in others a few Soviet experts were still functioning.

There were three striking aspects of Soviet aid to People's China. First, no political strings were attached. The aid was provided as a gesture of friendship to a socialist neighbor country. It was paid for on an agreed basis with exported Chinese products. Second, there was no permanent occupation of China by Soviet personnel. Soviet experts did not settle down in China. They did not take over the Chinese economy. Soviet experts went to China as specialists go to any piece of work, made their contribution and then went home with good feelings on both sides. Third, the relations between the Soviet Union and People's China were civilian, not military, nor was there any occupation of China by Soviet military personnel.

Soviet aid to People's China was urgently needed by the Chinese. At the outset the economic and military strength of the Soviet Union were greater than that of People's China. There is no suggestion that the Soviet Union took advantage of this superiority.

Soviet aid to People's China went far beyond supplying urgently needed materials and human skills. It established a new pattern in international relations,—a pattern of considerable importance. In carrying out their program of aid to the Chinese People's Republic the Soviet Government presented to the entire world a noteworthy example of the consideration, efficacy and restraint with which socialist states can aid one another.

3. "OUR FRIENDS FROM THE SOVIET UNION"

Soviet aid and cultural exchange are deeply appreciated in People's China. Throughout the whole population, from the oldest to the youngest, this appreciation is felt. In Peking on one wintry day we met a score of children walking with two nursery school teachers. The rosy-cheeked youngsters, three or four years of age, bundled in padded jackets, were having an afternoon's outing at the zoo. Some of them were clustered around their teachers, others were wandering along nonchalantly by themselves, singing and humming as they walked. The group was so fetching that we stopped to watch it go by. When the children saw us they called out in Chinese, "Hello, Auntie! Hello, Uncle!" In a moment we were surrounded. One small boy approached us gravely, put his hand in ours, and asked, "Are you our friends from the Soviet Union?" We were strangers; we were friendly. The little chap put two and two together and concluded that we must be from the Soviet Union.

Foreigners have not always been given the hand of friendship in China. In 1927 many Chinese who passed us on the streets of Canton gritted their teeth, glowered, and looked as though they would enjoy running us out of town. Through a hundred years the Chinese suffered aggression, intervention, invasion, occupation and humiliation. At the time of the First Opium War China was an independent, sovereign, almost self-sufficient country. Sixty years later, after foreign troops had suppressed the Boxer Rebellion, China was occupied by armed men in foreign uniforms and under foreign command. From 1932 to 1943 Japanese armed forces moved from city to city, taking over military control of China.

Foreigners collected Chinese customs and deposited them in foreign-owned banks. Foreigners were masters in Chinese ports. Foreigners held special concession areas where they established their businesses, set up their governments, maintained their own police forces and their courts, and enforced their own laws. The concessions were inhabited chiefly by Chinese who were the menials and did the hard work. Economic and political decisions were made by tiny minorities of foreigners. Outside a park in their own city of Shanghai we saw in 1927 the insulting sign: "Chinese and dogs keep out."

Remnants of this Age of Humiliation persist today in Hong Kong, a British Crown Colony. More than 2,000,000 Chinese live in Hong Kong, together with some 20,000 foreigners,—a ratio of 100 to 1. Yet the Governor, who has supreme and arbitrary power over the Colony and its inhabitants, is British and is appointed in London. There is no popular franchise. The police are under British control. A British army occupies the Colony. Before 1943 all foreign concessions in China were operated on this same colonial pattern.

Hong Kong and Taiwan, occupied by the armed forces of foreign powers, are remnants and examples of the position which the imperialists held in China before 1943, when foreign warships were stationed in Chinese harbors and patrolled Chinese navigable rivers. Today, a United States fleet patrols the narrow waterway separating the island of Taiwan from the remainder of China. Taiwan is occupied by the Nationalists, a defeated faction in the Chinese civil war. Their army is financed and supplied by the government of the United States. Fragments of the Nationalist's army are located on two islands, Quemoi and Matsu, which are within gunshot of the Chinese mainland. Yet if the Peking Government attempts to take back the islands, which are part of China, the Congress in Washington has authorized the President to make war on the Chinese People's Republic.

Most foreigners had gone to China merely asking permission to trade. They had then settled down, taken possession, and dictated where necessary at gun-point. With British, Germans and Russians the experience had been the same. The foreigners issued orders. The Chinese, living in their own country, disobeyed the orders issued by foreigners at the peril of their lives.

Against this century-old experience, the Chinese reacted with bitter anti-foreignism. Three times they took up arms and attempted to expel the invaders.—in the Taiping Revolution of 1851-64, in the Boxer Rebellion of 1899-1900, and in the struggle against foreign intervention that began in 1932 and ended with the Liberation of 1949.

After Liberation, certain foreign governments and foreign peoples came to China's aid. Heading the procession was China's ancient enemy, Russia. The Russia of the empire-building Tsars had been changed into a Soviet Russia committed to replace imperialism and colonialism by socialism and communism.

When Chairman Mao and his colleagues, after Liberation, went to Moscow to sign a treaty of peace and mutual aid, the imperialist West was gleeful. "Now," said they, "we will see the Russian Bear swallow a neighbor country." Had the Soviet Union been following the policy which dominated the history of recent centuries, this would have been the time to grab and assimilate China. The Soviet Union was strong. China was weak. Here was an ideal opportunity for the strong to drive a hard bargain which would convert the weaker party into a dependency or a sphere of influence.

What misgivings must have been in the hearts of many Chinese as spokesmen for the People's Government met the representatives of their former enemy from the North, sat down around a conference table, and after prolonged negotiations signed a treaty of peace and friendship. What was this, the sceptics must have asked, but the camel's head, pushed under the tent flap? A century earlier, other Westerners had come in the name of peace and friendship, only to take over the economic and political control of the country. This had been the common practice of all Westerners who had dealt with Asians. Would not this new venture result in a repetition of an old and abhorrent experience?

Events during the past decade have provided an object lesson, not only to the Chinese people, but to the entire world. The West has been amazed. The people of China have been reassured. The grab-and-keep pattern is not the touchstone of Russian foreign policy. Instead of smashing or subordinating a potential rival, the Soviet Government and people have done everything in their power to build up Chinese economy, strengthen the Chinese State and promote the success of the all-important Chinese First Five Year Plan. How does Moscow explain and justify such a policy? The answer is clear and emphatic: "We do not consider People's China a rival. We are neighbors and partners, both striving to build a socialist world."

A Chinese capitalist who was cooperating with the Peking Government was recently asked, "Does Russia control China?" "Russia does not control China any more than China controls Russia," was the answer. "We are both socialist nations. China has a lot to learn from Russia; it is helping

226

us to build. Honestness and sincerity are its policy. Now, after experience, I believe in unselfish assistance. We are making automobiles and airplanes which would not have been possible without the assistance of our Russian friends. Russian technical men have been quiet and unassuming. For that reason the Chinese like them. There is never the attitude of 'I am your master and we are helping you.' " *

This most recent experience which the Chinese people have had in their dealings with foreigners, and especially with those from the Soviet Union, has been reflected in the study of foreign languages. For generations foreigners had come to China and spoken their native tongues,—English, German, Japanese. If the Chinese wished to get on with the foreigners, to take and execute their orders, it was up to the Chinese to learn the language of the intruders. Consequently, many Chinese had learned European and other foreign languages. This was particularly true among Chinese business men in the seaports. As the British were the dominant power in the south (Hong Kong) and in Shanghai and the Yangtse valley, English was widely used and spoken there. Shop signs were in English. So were street signs and the direction-markers on street cars and busses.

Since Liberation a new policy has been adopted. Chinese is the official language. Business is done in that language and signs are painted in Chinese characters. Even hotels which cater to foreigners have their names in Chinese on the outside, and the floors are numbered in Chinese on the elevator shafts.

Soviet and other foreign technicians, coming by the thousands to People's China, created a demand for interpreters and translators. The popularity of "our friends from the Soviet Union" created interest in their language. A new for-

* *The Churchman,* February, 1958, pp. 12-13.

eign language pattern appeared in the schools. Before Liberation English was the popular taught language in Chinese middle and higher schools. After 1950, it changed to Russian.

When we were in Peking, the Institute of Foreign Languages had 800 students, half of whom were studying English and the other half were studying German, French and Spanish. At the same time, 5,000 students were studying Russian in a special institute set up to handle the influx into that foreign language field.

In Chinese middle schools, as in the institutions at college level, Russian was the preferred language in 1957. In Shanghai we were told that 95 percent of middle school students were electing Russian, while less than 5 percent elected English. In one of the middle schools we visited English had been dropped several years earlier as a language elective because there was no demand for it. In the 1958 study course, English was to be re-introduced into the school because several students wished to take it. As soon as qualified teachers could be found, English classes would be organized.

One foreign language was required of students in the Shanghai College of Finance and Economy. Before Liberation, English was a required subject in this college, with German and Japanese elective. In 1952 the college was reorganized with a strong emphasis on socialist content. Japanese was dropped. In December, 1957, when we were there, 12 classes were being held in Russian and 3 in English.

This academic revolution in foreign language study reflects not merely the shift in Chinese political alliances but also a transformation in Chinese popular interests and preferences. Until quite recently the Chinese placed the United States at the top of the list of China's friends. Today the United States occupies a position toward the bottom of the list and the Soviet Union is in first place.

United States public officials spent the years after 1949 denouncing the Peking regime and misrepresenting developments in China. There were two paths ahead of humanity, these spokesmen announced,—the path to freedom and the path to slavery. The Chinese people were following the path to slavery. There were two kinds of people in the world, they said,—children of light and children of darkness. The Chinese were among the children of darkness.

Such statements were duly reported in the Chinese press and over the Chinese radio. Slowly but surely, good will (which had been widespread in China after Washington's conversion of the Boxer indemnity money into scholarships which enabled Chinese students to study in the United States) was rapidly dissipated. United States and British participation in the Korean War and the general support given by the State Department to the Dutch in Indonesia, and the French in Indochina and North Africa, lined up the United States with the imperialists against the colonials, thus undermining still further the confidence which the Chinese people had felt in the good intentions of Washington.

Since all aspects of imperialism were ferociously unpopular in China after 1949, a good-will vacuum was created into which the Soviet Union stepped with socialist aid and friendship, cultural interchange and trade. The two big socialist neighbors became friends and fellow workers in building a socialist society.

Thus was created a new pattern in international relations. Instead of the rivalry, fear, suspicion and hatred that characterized the relations of the Western powers with one another through centuries of competitive empire building, these two builders of socialism turned to cooperation, sympathy, mutual confidence and friendship. A new formulation had been achieved in theory and applied to foreign relations in practice. From each nation according to its possibilities, to each nation according to its needs. This was assistance without domination or subversion, aid without strings.

4. HANDS AROUND THE WORLD

Destructive and disastrous wars fought after 1914 had several important effects on world thinking. *First,* they aroused an all but universal, popular desire to prevent another armed conflict, to disarm, and to abolish war as an instrument of foreign policy. *Second,* they led to a growing awareness that the suspicion, fear, hatred and the spirit of vengeance which are by-products of war-making are corrosive forces which eat away the vitals of a society. A community which wishes to survive and prosper must replace these negative and destructive forces by understanding, confidence and friendship. *Third,* suspicion, fear, hatred and the spirit of vengeance are not the normal products of "human nature," nor are they even dominant human characteristics. Very young children who have been reared in an atmosphere of security and love do not display them. Instead of being inborn, suspicion, fear, hatred and the spirit of vengeance are acquired and cultivated, either as a result of circumstance or as the product of propaganda and indoctrination. *Fourth,* people the world over are waking up to the fact that peace and friendship are impossible unless there is mutual knowledge, based on interchange not only of goods and services but of ideas, ideals and techniques. *Fifth,* contact and interchange are difficult or impossible unless peoples are able to cross the barriers of language.

A student in the Foreign Language Institute in Tashkent

said to us, "How can we hope to build peace unless there is friendship? How can we have friendship unless there is contact and interchange? We must cross the frontiers, see for ourselves and compare our ideas with those of our neighbors. We would be snobbish and arrogant if we demanded that all of our neighbors and visitors spoke our language. For the time being, we must learn their languages and hope that they will learn ours, until we all mature sufficiently to agree upon a common world language which all cultured human beings will speak, read and write."

Foreign travel is one of the ways in which the Soviet people, old and young, will realize this hope for contact and friendship. In Bombay, in February 1957, we met a party of Russian tourists visiting India. In Irkutsk airport, in late December 1957, we talked with a boy and two girls, students in the English department of the local Foreign Language Institute, who were going to England on an exchange basis, for six weeks, to study and to travel. A United States-Soviet agreement, signed in January, 1958, provided for a wide range of cultural exchange, including students, doctors, dancers, musicians, scientists. Horizons are widening all over the socialist world, and particularly for young people.

Immense collections of books, monographs, pamphlets and periodicals in foreign languages, their translation and distribution, coupled with the widespread development of foreign language teaching, are looked upon as forms of cultural interchange that will keep people in one nation or one part of the world informed concerning achievements and developments elsewhere. Similarly, music, the fine arts, games, sports and hobbies are crossing frontiers with mutual advantages to all parties.

Before history began, human beings were bartering and trading the products of their handiwork. Such exchanges of goods and services broke down many a barrier which otherwise would have proved impassable. Today the exchange of ideas, formulas, scientific information, inventions, blue prints and models are supplementing trade and commerce as a method of interchange between nations and peoples. One of the most important agreements made between the Soviet Union and People's China provided that each party should receive specific information concerning inventions, discoveries and technological developments in the other country.

Until two hundred years ago a manufacturing nation like Britain prohibited the export of machinery, designs and plans that would make it possible for competitors to break into the world markets which British manufacturers had developed for the products of their revolutionary new power machinery. Even today, patents and copyrights are protected by national law and international agreement against unauthorized use. But these same competing nations are willing and even eager to exchange and pool information dealing with the weather or with the antarctic land mass.

Socialist countries like the Soviet Union and People's China exchange technological information as readily as capitalist nations exchange weather reports. In a socialist world an invention or discovery that will raise the level of human well-being will be common property to be used for the benefit of peoples everywhere.

As varied interests, special skills and novel ideas develop new techniques, reveal nature's secrets and increase human control over the material universe and over the organization and direction of human endeavor, they establish a world culture, shared by human beings without reference to nationality, language, color, class or creed. Thus a culture pattern develops which is neither regional, national, nor partisan. It belongs to humanity.

At some point in their development, human relations crystallize into institutions. Through the ages communication, commerce, travel, migration and war have led to treaties, alliances, conquests and consolidation into power blocs. On one side there were spheres of influence, dependencies, colonies. On the other side were the empire builders, elbowing one another for a place in the sun and engaging, sooner or later, in wars of survival and elimination during which the more wealthy and powerful swallowed up their poorer and weaker neighbors.

"Growing specialization in production is increasing interdependence," said an experienced Asian social scientist to us. "Look at your own America. A century ago economists were writing about self-sufficiency. For them a continent such as North America, with its rich endowment of natural resources and its elaborate industrial organization, spelled independence of the remainder of the world. North American resources are still abundant, but with each advance in technology, the United States has become more dependent on other parts of the planet, until today it is producing and exporting a flood of manufactured articles which are being sold and used in practically every country. In exchange for these exports, your country is receiving six or eight billion dollars worth of metals, minerals, fibres, foods and some manufactured goods. North America is far more dependent on the outside world in 1958 than it was in 1858."

Our friend added: "What is true for the United States is even more evident in countries with limited natural resources, such as Britain, Germany and Japan. Mass production has imposed upon the modern world a degree of interdependence undreamed of in the days when home agriculture

233

provided for the simpler needs of populations still employing handicrafts and primitive factory industries in the production of consumer goods.

"These forces about which I have been speaking are compulsive," our friend continued. "An automotive industry requires petroleum, rubber, copper, tin and chrome. Even a top-ranking industrial country like the United States imports all of these products because they are all essential for its output of manufactures and they do not exist in sufficient quantities in the home territory.

"On the other side of the picture are historical factors of a different character. Experience has led men to question the wisdom of surrendering the destiny of a community to competition. There is not a 'free enterprise' country in which competition is free. Quite the contrary, regulations and governmental restrictions have developed across the entire free enterprise economy. Beyond the limitations which the free enterprisers themselves have imposed upon their own economies in the form of trade agreements, monopoly controls, tariffs, subsidies and other regulatory measures, is the experience in mutual aid and cooperation amassed by the third of mankind which has deposed competition and enthroned cooperation as the dominant motivating force in their communities. Cooperation and mutual aid are working, and working successfully, in the New World. Their value as binding forces in the life of peoples no longer rests upon theory, but upon the results of daily practice. Humanity is today presented with a choice: capitalism, with competition dominant, or socialism, with cooperation dominant; hit-and-run for profit versus the rational use of science and technology to raise the levels of human culture."

One of the essential tasks, and certainly one of the most urgent tasks of socialism will be the abolition of the war pattern, in both theory and practice. Until that task is achieved, human society will be torn asunder periodically by military conflicts which destroy property, snuff out human life, disrupt inter-community relationships and lay the foundations for future suspicion, fear and hatred.

Nowhere in our travels, east and west, were we under the necessity of pointing out the dangers of a third general war or even of the local wars which have disturbed and distorted public relations since 1945. Those whom we met took the words out of our mouths. "We must end war and make peace," they insisted. Their thoughts ran like this: "War in the past was hideous but tolerable. It was not total; it afflicted directly only a small part of any community. Nations could make war and still have a reasonable chance to survive. Even before 1945, however, the damage done to human beings and to communities by mechanized warfare had passed the level of tolerance. This fact led to the outbreak of revolutions during both the 1914-18 and the 1939-45 wars. But after the development of atomic weapons and their testing on the helpless populations of Hiroshima and Nagasaki, war became impossible. Henceforth men must face the basic choice: Disarm or die. Subsequent development of nuclear weapons with vastly greater destructive potentials merely underscore the impossibility of another general war."

What was the alternative? World organization, of course. Since the interdependent nations had become in fact one world, the next logical step was to accept the fact and establish it as an axiom of world law. However, this was easier said than done. The negative position, of opposing imperialism and war, was accepted enthusiastically by East Europeans, Asians and Africans. The positive position of a federation of socialist states, or of the appointment of a commission to make an exhaustive inquiry into the possibilities of such a development, was generally branded as impracticable.

We raised this question with many persons in the New World. Their answers were almost everywhere the same. They said that this step might be taken some day, but the time was not yet ripe. They insisted that the surging nationalism of the past two decades, centered about independence and self-determination, would tolerate no interference, especially not the restraints imposed by a strong world authority. Finally they argued that socialism is not yet sufficiently developed to take a step beyond the nation to the inter-nation. "The socialist countries now have a consultative economic committee working to regularize economic relations within the group of nations building socialism," said some experts, with whom we talked. "Beyond that point the socialist countries are not yet prepared to go. Their present requirements can be met by treaties, trade agreements and working commissions."

World federation has been dreamed about and talked about through the centuries. Recent developments in transportation and communication, by converting the planet into a neighborhood, have posed the question of establishing a world authority to deal with the manifold problems which world integration has thrown into the lap of modern man.

Treaties and alliances had pointed toward world integration. After the Hague Conference of 1899, one attempt after another had been made to subordinate national boundaries to human welfare and establish international if not planetwide authority. First the League of Nations and then the United Nations had covenanted and agreed by charter to disarm, and end war. By 1958, the United Nations, with 82 members, was representative of world opinion and world interests to a degree never achieved by previous international organizations.

Still the authority vested in the League and in the United Nations was insufficient to enable these organizations to prevent war and stabilize peace, because a half dozen wealthy and powerful nations, equipped with the techniques of mechanized warfare, were stronger than the central authority and could, with impunity, ignore its decisions.

Imperialist forces which were in complete control of the League of Nations and which, working in unison were usually able to push their measures through the United Nations, recognized and upheld a pattern of national sovereignty which blocked any genuine effort to put effective checks on the right of individual nations to initiate and wage wars or to establish a world economic authority to deal with such vital issues as the use of natural resources, international trade, communication and finance. Competitive nationalism refused to tolerate any such interference with the sovereignty of individual nations.

Such a conclusion was derived from the accepted principles of national sovereignty as well as from the practices of international relations and international law during recent centuries. If the theory and the practices of the competitive struggle for wealth and power makes it impossible for mankind to reach hands around the planet and establish the practices and the institutional forms necessary to maintain peace and friendship, one of the greatest services which the builders of socialism can render to the human race is the inauguration of a workable world federation.

Through thousands of years localism, ignorance and prejudice, fostered by circumstances beyond the control of local populations, have kept the human family divided, competitive and periodically at war. With the coming of one world, and with an organization capable of administering that one world in a manner calculated to advance the interests of all its citizens, hands are being reached around the world with the increasing assurance that they will be grasped by other hands, representing other places which have joined in the common endeavor to end war and erect a worldwide culture as a scaffolding by means of which human brotherhood can be successfully established.

5. "TELL THE PEOPLE OF AMERICA"

Some of the most enlightening experiences in our journeys around the world, particularly in socialist countries, were the messages given us for the American people. We travel as students, observers, writers, as teachers, as workers for peace and friendship between nations, peoples and members of the human family. Since we are not public servants and have no connection with the government of the United States beyond our citizenship, we cannot carry messages of an official nature. Nor can our hosts in foreign countries speak for their governments, since they also are not public officials.

Many friends in the United States gave us messages to take to the peoples in Russia and the East. Even more people in Russia and China gave us messages for the American people. As man to man, woman to woman, writer to writer, scientist to scientist, teacher to teacher, peace worker to workers for peace, such messages to the people in the United States could be sent and are here being delivered.

Diplomats have their province and function. They have been at their posts for centuries. Particularly in recent years, with the multiplication of international contacts and the expansion of diplomatic and consular services, representatives of governments have numerous opportunities to communicate with one another. Yet the history of the past half century is so filled with records of misunderstanding, tension and conflict that people the world over have lost faith in the possibilities of diplomacy as an effective means of preventing armed struggle, of maintaining the peace, and promoting friendship.

"With diplomats on the job," new friends said to us at a meeting in Azerbaijan, "we get crises, ultimatums, wars. So far as we can find out, the people of America do not want war. Certainly we here in this country do not want it. If only the people could get together, they could come to an understanding, abolish war, disarm, and spend the billions now going into the arms race for the uplift of living standards and the promotion of cultural exchanges.

"We feel this very strongly. We do not want another war. We are sure that your people are of the same mind. Tell them from us, in the name of this meeting, that we want to live at peace with all men. If we have problems, let us analyze them. If we have differences of interest or of opinion, let us get together, discuss them and find ways in which the differences can be settled without the need of burning and killing. We are not sure about your government. We do not meet or know your politicians and statesmen. But we have met you and we believe that you stand for peace and friendship. Tell the peace-loving, friendly people in America what we think and how we feel."

When we parted with our new friends in one country after another, they repeated such sentiments in various languages and with varying degrees of emphasis and urgency. Usually those who had suffered the most war loss were the most anxious to reach people in potential enemy territory and make known their feelings. Wherever we went, with whomsoever we talked, the emphasis was on peace.

239

One would expect that a public meeting devoted to broadening peace and friendship might pass a resolution directed to a like organization in the West. Similarly, at a public dinner or reception it would be in order to drink the health or convey messages to men and women beyond the frontiers. This occurred at all dinners and parties we attended. But who would expect a middle-aged woman with a kerchief over her head to step up to us on the street in front of a suburban Uzbek school we were visiting and to say, "They tell me you are from America. Is that so?" Then, as we assented, she went on, "I am glad to meet you. Never before have I had a chance to talk with any Americans. When you go back home, tell the American people, from me, and from us here in this town, that we want peace, and we want them to know that we stand for peace. We have been through war. We know its terrors. War is bad. We should never have another war. Tell that to the people of the United States."

Her words tumbled forth as she poured out her pent-up thoughts. "Another thing you should tell them. We are not only opposed to a war in which we would try to harm the people of America and they would try to harm us. Of course we are against such a war. But our feeling for the American people is very much more than a desire to avoid war with them. We admire the American people because they have stood up in the past for freedom and brotherhood. We also are for freedom and brotherhood. We feel that they are our brothers and sisters, so we want to live with them in peace and in friendship."

We had an opportunity to talk at length with a steel worker in Leningrad who said much the same thing to us. "When you go back to your homes," he said, "tell the American people that we feel no ill-will against them because of the actions of their government. There are times when

240

peoples and their governments get very far apart. We believe that such is the case now in the United States. We wish that this were not true. We would like to be friends with the American people and with their government. But if that is not possible, we would rather be close to the people than to the government, because people are more constant than governments. Governments change. People remain much the same.

"I have read some history. I know that not long ago there was a revolution in the United States against the government of that period. In those days we Russians were not, in the main, revolution-conscious. Nevertheless there were many in Russia who were glad when the people of the English colonies in North America threw off the fetters of imperialism and declared themselves independent.

"Now the situation is reversed. It is we here in Russia who have revolted against Tsarist tyranny. You Americans as a people are no longer revolution-conscious. Nevertheless, we know that many of you in North America rejoiced with us when we made an end of Tsarism.

"We in the Soviet Union are attempting to build socialism,—the next step in historical progress. You in America are not yet ready to take that step. But already there are many Americans who are aware that this historical step from capitalism to socialism must be taken. When the happy day comes for your country to take that step the peoples of America will join the peoples of the Soviet Union and other sister republics in building socialism.

"Governments change," he said. "People remain much the same. So we look beyond the government of the United States to its people. We greet and salute them as our brothers in the cause of peace, freedom and socialism."

We were leaving the Baku Pioneer Palace and putting on

our coats in the hall when a group of children and their mothers surrounded us. After exchanging pins and coins and laughingly refusing one girl who insisted on giving us her fountainpen, we listened to their messages. "Will you tell American children that we would like to correspond with them?" they asked. "Will you give them our address: the Palace of Pioneers, Baku, Azerbaijan, USSR?" We promised to pass on the good word. They in turn promised to answer any letters that came. One of the mothers chimed in with hearty greetings to the mothers and housewives of America. "Tell them we wish them peace and friendship." This message also we are glad to transmit.

We were walking through a memorial park in Leningrad. Fresh flowers had been laid, in the bleak November weather, on the graves of those who died in the battle for the city. A working man came up and spoke to us in German. "You are foreigners," he said, shaking our hands heartily. "It does not matter from what country you come. Will you tell your people when you get home that above all we must have peace in the world. War is hell. Let's make heaven on earth, not hell." As we walked away, he stood and waved until we could see him no longer.

Several students at the University of Peking had entertained us delightfully and taken us on a tour of the campus. We ended our visit late in the afternoon. Our last call was to see a girls' dormitory. After the social rooms were shown we were asked, "Would you like to see a bedroom?" We knocked on a chance closed door and in the twilight found two girls sitting beside a table by the window eating peanuts. They jumped up, surprised by the unexpected visit, and when our party of five filed into the room hastily tried to sweep the peanut shells off the table and get chairs. We said, "Don't bother. We're here for just a minute and are sorry to disturb

242

you. May we sit on the couch?" Chairs were finally brought and the girls blushingly offered us fruit and nuts. We gathered around the table, shelled and ate peanuts while asking and answering questions.

"Tell us," the girls asked, "about university students in the United States. We did not meet the forty Americans who were here after the Moscow Youth Festival. How do American students live? How do they spend their spare time? Do they also eat peanuts? We have heard it is expensive to attend an American university. Cannot the children of workers and peasants get a university education?"

After some discussion and exchange of experiences they said to us, "We imagine that many American students would like to pay a visit to Peking University. Certainly we would enjoy having them come. And of course we would be more than pleased to visit your country and get into contact with students, student organizations and student life in the United States. What a fine thing it would be if a number of American students could come here each year and spend some time with us, while similar groups of Chinese students were visiting your country.

"How much better such an exchange would be than for these same young people to bomb and burn and destroy back and forth across the Pacific Ocean. We young people all want to live. We all want to learn. War will prevent us from learning and deprive many of us of the possibility of living. Peace and friendship make so much better sense."

Without exception the young people and students we met in People's China were curious about the United States. Without exception they were friendly. They disapproved Washington's attitude toward China and its support of the rebel government in Taiwan, but they believed that if the youth of America and Asia could meet face to face, they would be able to understand one another and would benefit from the contact.

There is a permanent agricultural exhibition in Moscow, —an immense affair covering many acres. Through the center of the exhibition grounds runs a broad thoroughfare, bordered on both sides with the buildings which house exhibits. Each of the fifteen republics composing the Soviet Union has erected its own building, true to its own style of architecture. Green parks and fountains fill the open spaces.

We went one blustery November afternoon to have a look at the exhibition. It had frozen hard and the outside vegetation that could be damaged by cold weather was limp. Inside the colorful buildings were cheering exhibits of fruits, vegetables, grains and nuts. What seemed like hills of oranges and apples and cabbages and carrots and lemons brought brightness to what had been a grey day outside. Many of the exhibition halls were decorated with flowers. We were especially delighted with a fine exhibition of chrysanthemums and spent some time examining and admiring them. As we were leaving this hall a young agronomist who worked in the building hurried out after us with two huge bouquets made up of some of the choicest blossoms. As he presented the flowers he made a courteous little speech, in English. "Please accept these tokens of the respect and affection in which we hold the people of America. We wish to be on good terms with them, to share the best of our culture with them in exchange for the best that their culture has to offer us. We want to join with them in a steadfast endeavor to establish and preserve peace and friendship on this earth." He bowed, smiled a friendly smile, and made a large request, "Please tell this to the people of America."

INDEX

245

246

247